The Secret Crab Island

by James P. Millard

Photo courtesy of Roger and Doug Harwood

America's Historic Lakes
P.O. Box 262
South Hero, Vermont 05486

The Secrets of Crab Island

First print edition
2004

This publication is a revised version of an original work published electronically on America's Historic Lakes in 2002.

Published by

America's Historic Lakes
P.O. Box 262
South Hero, Vermont 05486
http://www.historiclakes.org

ISBN Number 0-9749854-0-6
Printed in the United States of America

Table of Contents

Foreword

American Army Surgeon James Mann, who spent several weeks on Crab Island in the fall of 1814, described the island as "a barren uninhabited spot." Dr. Mann's experience tending to the wounded of the two mighty navies that clashed in Cumberland Bay on September 11, 1814 undoubtedly colored his feelings about the small island in Lake Champlain.

As James P. Millard illustrates in this volume, for such a barren uninhabited spot, Crab Island is a place rich in historical associations and secrets. Much of the island's history derives from its location in Lake Champlain, the strategic waterway that helped shape the course of North American empire in the colonial, revolutionary, and early national periods. In a vast and impenetrable wilderness of mountains and primeval forests, Europeans could conduct commerce or wage war only by using the natural highways formed by lakes and rivers. The "most important inland water in North America." was how a returned prisoner from Quebec referred to Lake Champlain on an early English map. The lake was "the key of the enemy's country, a canal leading from New England and New York to the very bowels of Canada." Vermont historian Ralph Nading Hill described Lake Champlain as "a silver dagger from Canada to the heartland of the American colonies that forged the destiny of France and England in America, and of the United States."

For someone with such a keen sense of history, it is surprising that Henry Adams did not express a greater interest in Lake Champlain. Shortly before leaving Harvard in 1877 to settle in Washington as an independent writer and scholar, Adams had shifted his attention to the study of American history. "History is a tangled skein that one may take up at any point, and break when one has unraveled enough," Adams wrote in his autobiography. His historical masterpiece, <u>History of the United States of America During the Administrations of Thomas Jefferson and James Madison</u>, an ambitious narrative account of America during the years 1801-1817, published in nine volumes between 1889 and 1891, makes scant mention of Crab Island.

Early in the last century, Adams wrote a revealing letter to Henry Osborne Taylor in which he tried to distinguish his approach to history from the approach of more traditional scholars. For Adams, accuracy was a relatively secondary concern; his primary concern was that his *ensemble* be in scale. "To me, accuracy is relative," Adams remarked, "I care very little whether my details are exact, if only my *ensemble* is in scale." However he warned Taylor not to follow his example: "You need to be thorough in your study and accurate in your statements," Adams cautioned.

Jim Millard's *ensemble* is in scale, the result of his thorough study, accurate statements, and old-fashioned hard work. Living near the shore of Lake Champlain on South Hero Island, he has shared the lake's changing moods and understands its rhythms. Jim knows his subject personally, having traveled all parts of Lake Champlain to gain new information and collect new images. <u>The Secrets of Crab Island</u> makes an important contribution to our understanding of Lake Champlain.

John Krueger
Clinton County Historical Association
Plattsburgh, New York

January 2004

Acknowledgements

This print edition, like the online version, is the result of the contributions of many individuals. Crab Island, I like to say, exerts an influence over those who visit her. That influence is borne witness to in the efforts of folks like Jim Bailey, Roger Harwood, and John Rock. It is also evident, I believe, in the efforts of us telling the story.

Nothing I have published, America's Historic Lakes would not exist, were it not for the loving support of my wife. Lynn has long ago become accustomed to my frequent absences into the office. She has also proved a patient proofreader and editor. Greg Furness has supplied me with materials from his research for many years now, this work, like much else published by America's Historic Lakes, is a product of his efforts. Roger Harwood has been my strongest supporter, not only by his encouragement, but by real, honest to goodness research. He and his brother Doug have provided many wonderful photographs, including almost all of the aerial photos. Roger is the person I count on to knock on doors and dig up that material I don't know how to get.

Local historians Jim Bailey, Addie Shields and Jim Hays have been very helpful. I'm particularly grateful to Jim Bailey for sharing his earlier work on Crab Island. I owe a debt of gratitude to Frank Pabst, John Tomkins III, John Rock, Linda Harwood, and Phil LaMarche. I sincerely appreciate the efforts of Dr. John Krueger, Executive Director of the Clinton County Historical Association, for his willingness to write the Foreword for this book. John and the CCHA are doing some wonderful work in the Plattsburgh area. I am proud to be associated with this organization.

I would like to extend my appreciation to Anthony and Helen Connolly, Cheryll Berg and Stephen Sutter for their support and assistance with the material about their ancestors' time on the island. They graciously allowed the use of the wonderful photos of their family on Crab Island.

I would be remiss if I didn't mention the staff at Durick Library at Saint Michael's College. And, finally, I would like to thank those New York State officials from DEC and OPRHP who have recognized the public's interest in this historic place and are now working to make things right for Crab Island and those fallen heroes who take their rest there.

Introduction

The Crab Island Monument. Photo by the author

Just outside of Plattsburgh, New York, south of Cumberland Bay and north of famous Valcour Island there sits a small, heavily wooded limestone isle. Fairly unremarkable in appearance, it has all that one would expect to find on one of the many islands in this deep and lovely lake- rocky shores covered with shale, mixed forests of conifers, maples and oaks, and great bunches of poison ivy growing profusely in the few open patches between shore and forest.

Yet, tiny Crab Island is different from many of its better-known sister islands. One of the keys to its difference lies in the small clearing on the northwestern shore- here one can find a tall granite obelisk, surrounded by a rusting fence.

 The monument does not tell why it stands- the bronze plaques that once adorned its sides are gone. The mighty granite eagles adorning two sides have had their heads broken off by vandals. The large granite blocks have gaping holes where mortar once held them together. Continuing our walk along the western shore, we notice an opening in the woods. To our right, leading down to the shore, is a large concrete ramp. It stops just short of the water's edge. Returning to our path, we notice a large stone chimney entangled in thick brush and trees. Closer observation shows the chimney culminates in a large fireplace set within the foundation of what was some sort of building. From the looks of this, it may very well have been a substantial structure. Might this be one of Crab Island's secrets?

A little further south one can find a small shed, not much bigger than an outhouse; the sole surviving building on Crab Island. Beyond this shed, there is a clearing with other signs of human activity. It is obvious someone has worked here on the island clearing the thick brush and poison ivy.

Undoubtedly by now most observers will have had their attention drawn to a large American Flag flapping majestically above the highest reaches of the pines and oaks to the south. The flag flies atop an unusual flagstaff; painted white, secured by massive steel cables. Why does *Old Glory* fly here, on this tiny island? Who erected this massive flagstaff, and what was their motivation?

Continuing down the Trillium and Jack-in-the-Pulpit bordered path we finally reach the southwestern shore. The shore is littered with sharp and jagged rock- shale and limestone- harboring more mystery.

Crab Island has many tales to tell. The monument, ramshackle shed, the flagpole in the clearing, and even the rocks on the shore are clues to its secrets. These are the *Secrets of Crab Island.*

Images of Crab Island, clockwise from top left:

Vandalized stone eagle from the Crab Island Monument, the only remaining building on the island, the rear of the monument as seen through the iron fence, stone fireplace at the ruins of the Caretaker's Cottage. Photos by the author.

Cephalopod fossil from Crab Island in Lake Champlain

Long before the great plate collisions that formed Vermont's rocks and mountains, ancient squid-like creatures, like this 450 million year old cephalopod, swam in the Iapetus Ocean.

On loan from the University of Vermont, Perkins Geology Museum.

Crab Island fossil on display at the ECHO Center in Burlington, Vermont. Photo by the author.

I. Prehistory: The Secrets of the Stones

Crab Island first began keeping her secrets some 450 million years ago. The region we now know as Lake Champlain was but a small part of a large, shallow, tropical sea. The region was warm and the waters teemed with ancient life. Vast coral reefs with all their colorful diversity, brachiopods (what we today would call shellfish), gastropods (snails), creatures strange and common- crinoids, cephalopods, bryozoans and trilobites were everywhere.[1]

The rocky south shore of Crab Island. The rocks along the shore abound with fossils. Photo by the author.

Hundreds of millions of years passed; continents collided, the Earth was in the midst of great upheaval. Great mountain ranges, much higher than we see today, sprang up on each side of what became a deep valley. The teeming ocean was forced away as the region literally rose from the depths of the Earth. The life that was within these seas was buried in the muck and mud of the valley. Over time, much time, this mud became limestone and shale. Crab Island, itself a limestone mountain, began to keep the first of her secrets; embedded within the rocks along her shores would be millions of fossils. These are vestiges of life from ancient oceans- hundreds of millions of years old.

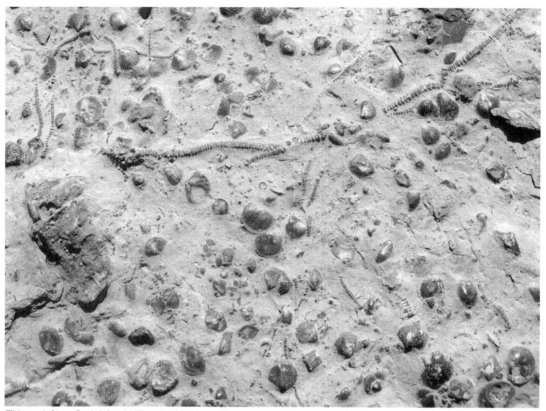

This rock from Crab Island still resembles an ancient seabed. Photo by the author.

Trilobite fossil from South Hero, Vermont. Photo by the author.

James G. Bailey in his "The Forgotten Graves of Crab Island" tells us that the island may have received its name from "a species of mollusk which a casual observer might easily mistake for crabs." [2] That is probably true, but this writer prefers to believe the name was chosen because of the abundance of fossils in the rocks along the shore. When I see a trilobite, I think of an ancient crab.

This planet is constantly in flux. The time humans have resided here is but an instant in the timeline of Earth's history. For hundreds of millions of years, the region was submerged under vast seas, hemmed in by the loftiest of mountains. Then, some 5 million years ago, the ice came.

Massive glaciers covered the region; the change could not have been more profound. Reaching at times to a depth of over a mile, these mighty sheets of ice scoured the earth to bedrock and depressed what earth remained beneath them. Then, a mere 20,000 or so years ago the great ice sheet began to recede. Slowly, the enormous glaciers melted, leaving behind a vast freshwater lake. These melt waters stayed in the region, held back from the sea by the mass of the huge glacier to the north. Some 15,000 years ago, Lake Vermont was formed .[3]

Lake Vermont wasn't here very long, in a geological sense. Within a couple of thousand years, the glaciers to the north had melted sufficiently to allow sea water to rush in to the area, depressed as it was by the sheer weight of the ice sheet that at one time covered it. The freshwaters of Lake Vermont gave way to the briny depths of the Champlain Sea. The rise of land we know as Crab Island in all likelihood projected out of an ocean once again.

Another cataclysmic change was in the making. Human beings would find their way to the shores of the Champlain Sea.

Crab Island would hold secrets anew.

Left: The southwestern shore of Crab Island. Right: Brachiopod fossils from Crab Island. Photos by the author.

Winter view towards Valcour and Crab Island from Sawyer Bay in South Hero, Vermont. Photo by the author.

Notes:

[1] Laurence R. Becker, State Geologist, Fossils of the Lake Champlain Region, 5 May 2002, <http://www.anr.state.vt.us/geology/pubint.htm> (16 May 2002)

[2] James G. Bailey, "THE FORGOTTEN GRAVES OF CRAB ISLAND" (The Antiquarian-Fall 1988, Allan Everest, Editor Clinton County Historical Association, Plattsburgh, NY) 1
also republished with permission: America's Historic Lakes, <http://www.historiclakes.org/ccha/bailey1.htm > May 2001

[3] Lake Champlain Maritime Museum, Geological History, <http://www.lcmm.org/site/harbor/resource_pages/timeline/geological.htm > (16 May 2002)

II. Habitation: The Arrival of the People of the Dawn

Lake Champlain sunrise, dawn breaks over the Green Mountains of Vermont. Photo by the author.

We do not know when the first human set foot on Crab Island. We do know the first people to inhabit the region arrived around 8,000-11,000 years ago, right about the time the Champlain Sea was giving way to what would become Lake Champlain.[1] We also know the region was very different from what we see today.

When the first humans arrived here (hunter/gatherers we now know as Paleo-Indians) Crab Island and the surrounding region was probably composed largely of tundra, with some areas of encroaching forest. Animals long-since vanished from the Earth walked the same ground as these early inhabitants. Mastodon, Wooly Mammoths and Caribou were plentiful and served as food to these early hunters.[2] We know Paleo-Indians inhabited the islands because traces of their existence have been found on the shores of Grand Isle, just across the water from Crab Island. Other sites have been located in the Ticonderoga region and near Highgate, Vermont.

By 7,000 B.C., the large mammals were extinct. The caribou herds had moved north, where they remain today. Forests increasingly predominated; the inhabitants of the

Lake Region were entering what is now called the Archaic period. Subsistence was still largely from hunting and gathering, but fishing took on an increasingly important role.[3] Dugout canoes were used for fishing and traveling up and down the lakes and streams.[4] Places occupied included the Otter Creek, Lamoille and Winooski River valleys, and an ever-increasing number of inhabitants lived in the northern reaches-along the Missisquoi and on the Isle la Motte. Along the western shore, humans also resided, but evidently not in as large a number as those in the east. The lake eventually came to be known as a boundary line between different tribal groups.

By the start of the Woodland period, some 1,000-2,000 years ago, agriculture had taken hold. Thriving settlements were established at places like East Creek near present day Orwell, Winooski, near Burlington, and Missisquoi, close by Swanton. Pottery was in use. Remnants have been found at all of these locations. The inhabitants became more clearly distinct in their tribal affiliations. The western shore was the home of the Iroquoian tribes, and the Abenaki (Algonquian) peoples resided to the east of the great lake. We can be fairly sure that natives from each group would have stopped off at Crab Island in their travels, perhaps having to take refuge from a storm. Abenaki tribal legend tells of Odzihozo, a much smaller island to the south, where the great "Transformer" took his rest after creating the lakes.

The tribes engaged in conflicts among themselves. The Iroquois and Abenaki, especially, at times harbored great enmity for each other. Populations along the lake waned and increased largely due to these wars among the early inhabitants. The suffering that the native people experienced at the hands of each other, however, was nothing compared to what they were to know at the hands of the white man.

Notes:

[1] William A. Haviland, Marjory W. Power, "The Original Vermonters: Native Inhabitants, Past and Present" (University of Vermont: Published by University Press of New England, Hanover, NH: 1994) 14-19

[2] Ibid. 25-28

[3] Ibid. 38

[4] Ibid. 83

III. Conflict: The Coming of the Europeans

On July 4, 1609, an inauspicious event occurred at Crab Island. Several small vessels passed the island headed south up the lake. Of itself, this would not have seemed noteworthy. After all, travelers had been journeying the great lake for millennia.

Aboard these vessels were white men, European discoverers seeing the great waters for the first time. Had they simply been on a journey of discovery that would have been one thing. These men, however, were planning to do battle with an enemy they had never seen.

Samuel de Champlain, together with 2 other whites and about 60 Algonquian Indians, continued south, exploring both sides of the lake until they reached the Crown Point or Ticonderoga peninsula. Here, in a bitter and one-sided battle, the Europeans and their native companions routed the Iroquois they had come to purposely to defeat. The Iroquois, stung by these strange newcomers and their terrible new weapons, would never forget what happened that fateful day. The stage was set for a long and bitter conflict between the French and their native allies and their enemies to the south who would ally themselves with the Iroquois.

Île St. Michel, Nouvelle-France

The French established themselves in the north, calling this land New France. To the south, the English had settled in abundance. This was New England to them. Each side claimed parts of this region for its sovereign. The native people, who had lived here for millennia, were largely discounted, except for their value as allies in war. Unfortunately, for them, they often took sides in the white man's conflicts. They also suffered terribly from the white man's diseases. Whole villages were wiped out by strange new maladies from which the natives had no natural immunity.

By 1640 the French were sending their missionaries up and down the lakes. Serving God and King, it was their mission to convert the "savages" and enlist them in the service of the French king. Tiny Crab Island would have borne witness to countless canoe trips by the Black Robes, as they were called. Isaac Jogues himself, now a Catholic saint, may have stopped off at the island.

In July 1666 the French had erected a fort on Isle la Motte, some miles northeast of Crab and Valcour Islands. Here they had a staging ground for what were to be a series of incursions against their Iroquois enemies to the south and west. A long period of bloody warfare ensued, with one expedition after another traveling up and down the lake, with only one real objective in mind- death and destruction. These raids were

usually conducted in the dead of winter, in conditions almost unimaginable to us today. Marching on snowshoes past Crab Island, the French and their Abenaki allies and the Iroquois raiders heading north would travel the frozen lake and beyond, often hundreds of miles, to strike their foes in stealthy guerilla warfare.

View across the frozen lake towards Crab and Valcour Islands. Photo by the author.

Our little island, named by the French St. Michel, witnessed one conflict after another. The local wars between the native peoples gave way to bloody battles between the Europeans. In time, the settlers from each far away land would claim the lake for its sovereign. King William's War, Dummer's War, Queen Anne's War, King George's War, and the French and Indian War would all take place upon the lake in the span of less than 75 years.

Yet, Crab Island's most significant role in the region's history was yet to come.

IV. Incident at Cliff Haven: October 12, 1759

Warfare in earnest came to the shores of Crab Island in October, 1759. Lake Champlain and Lake George had figured prominently in this bloody conflict. The waterways continued in their vital role as the only means of transport through the wilderness. Combatants had traveled past the island in massive armadas and solitary native canoes. Now, as this latest conflict was drawing to its dramatic conclusion, the sheltered bays off Crab Island were to witness a dramatic event that would leave its secrets hidden for over 200 years.

By September 1759, the French presence on the lakes had been greatly reduced. Forts Carillon and St. Frederic had been abandoned to the British. Lord Jeffrey Amherst was driving relentlessly north towards Canada, determined to erase the last vestiges of French power from the lakes. The French determined to make a stand at Île-aux-Noix in the Richelieu River. It was deemed critical to stop the British juggernaut from advancing down the river towards Montreal and Quebec.

Despite having lost the forts to the south, the French were still a formidable threat to Amherst's plan. Still in possession of a naval force of some size, the French could make things very difficult as Amherst drove towards the north with his army. Any vessel had to navigate the narrow stretches of the lake. Attacks from armed vessels could do much damage to ships loaded with troops. Lord Jeffrey knew he had to destroy the French fleet.

Setting out on the afternoon of October 11 from Crown Point, Amherst's fleet consisted of the 155-ton, 20-gun brig *Duke of Cumberland*, 115-ton, 16-gun sloop *Boscawen*, 6-gun radeau *Ligonier* and several bateaux and row galleys.[1]

The French naval force was made up of the schooner *La Vigilante*, 10 4 and 6 pounders and swivels, and three unusual sloop-like vessels called xebecs. Named for fish found in the region, the *La Masquinongé*, *La Brochette*, and *L'Esturgeon*, carried an assortment of armament, some of it captured from the British at Fort William Henry by Montcalm in 1757.[2]

The British fleet was separated early on, the brig and sloop easily outdistancing the cumbersome radeau, bateaux and row galleys. Rowing all night long, the crew of one of the bateaux became confused and ended up being captured by the French near the Four Brothers Islands. Fighting contrary winds, the British on the rest of these small vessels ended up spending the next five days at Ligonier Bay near Willsboro. Meanwhile, the larger sailing vessels continued their search for the French ships. After much maneuvering off the coast of Grand Isle and running aground near Bixby and Young Island, the British finally caught sight of the French xebecs entering Cumberland Bay. *La Vigilante* had escaped and was hiding near Isle la Motte, anxiously awaiting the other less maneuverable vessels. They would never arrive.

French fleet commander D'Olabaratz [a.k.a. *de la Bras*] called a hasty council with the captains of the other two vessels. They were anchored in the narrow channel between Crab Island and the New York shore. The awkward xebecs would never be able to out maneuver the British vessels. Under the best of conditions they were difficult to sail. The fickle winds of Cumberland Bay put them in a hopeless position.

The decision was made to scuttle the three ships and escape on foot to Canada. Hurriedly, the masts were cut, and cannons, swivels and other armament were thrown overboard. Other cannons were spiked to render them useless. The French crew fled through the forest towards Canada. Nine days later, they arrived at Île-aux-Noix.

The next morning the British arrived off the shores of Crab Island. Amherst landed some of his troops on the island; he may have come ashore himself. *La Masquinongé* was the least damaged of the three vessels, having been run aground rather than sunk. She was repaired and taken as a prize to join the British fleet. By October 26 the vessel, renamed the *Amherst*, was at Crown Point. She was now in the service of His Britannic Majesty. The next day, the *Boscawen*, *Amherst* and some 200 men in bateaux were sent to raise the two remaining vessels from the depths off Cliff Haven and Crab Island. Successful in their attempt to raise the ships, these sloops also became part of Amherst's fleet.[3]

Much of the armament from the vessels had wisely been thrown overboard. Vessels could be raised, it was another thing to locate and raise guns from the depths. For another 209 years, these guns would lay hidden in the channel between Crab Island and the high cliffs of the New York shore.

Finally, in September 1968, three young divers found the cannons along with several anchors, a large swivel gun, muskets and a saber.

Unfortunately, some of the artifacts did not receive necessary treatment for their preservation after such a long period in the lake. The muskets and the saber were severely damaged as a result. The swivel gun was eventually placed in the Clinton

County Historical Museum. One of the impressive cannons is on display at Clinton County Community College on Bluff Point in Plattsburgh. The other resides in Crown Point, New York at the Crown Point State Historical Site.[4]

Crab Island as seen from Cliff Haven. Photo by the author.

Left: British 12-pounder from La Masquinongé at Crown Point State Historical Site. This cannon is believed to have been captured by the French during the Battle of Fort William Henry. [5] Photo by the author.

Notes:

[1] Russell P. Bellico, "Sails and Steam in the Mountains: A Maritime and Military History of Lake George and Lake Champlain" (Purple Mountain Press, Fleischmanns, NY: Revised Edition 2001) 98

[2] André Charbonneau "The Fortifications of Île aux Noix" (Ottawa, Parks Canada 1994) Appendix A: 331, 332

[3] Russell P. Bellico, "Sails and Steam in the Mountains: A Maritime and Military History of Lake George and Lake Champlain" (Purple Mountain Press, Fleischmanns, NY: Revised Edition 2001) 100, 101

[4] Ibid. 110, 111

[5] James T. Hays, David E. Mize, and Richard W. Ward, "Guns under Lake Champlain" (York State Tradition, Spring 1969) 18

V. The American Revolution

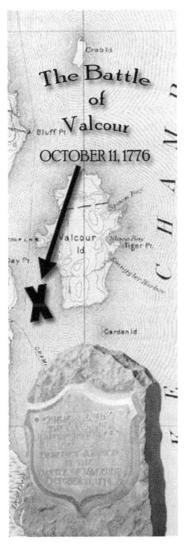

The Battle of Valcour
OCTOBER 11, 1776

After a brief period of relative peace on the lakes after the end of the French and Indian War, conflict returned to the waterways. No longer were the American colonists concerned about France as an enemy. This time, Britain herself would become the chief antagonist. The strategic importance of the Richelieu River/Lake Champlain/Lake George corridor would again weigh heavily in this conflict.

By 1775 open rebellion had erupted in New England. Lake Champlain was the scene of some of the first major incidents of the Revolution. On May 10, Ethan Allen, Benedict Arnold and the Green Mountain Boys seized Ticonderoga in a daring raid. The following day Seth Warner and Remember Baker captured the token British force at Crown Point. With one stroke, the weak British presence on Lake Champlain had been eliminated. Caught unaware, the Crown had left open an invasion route to Canada. The rebels would soon exploit this opening.

Crab Island, probably still known by the name given it by the French- St. Michel, lay along the route of one major military expedition after another. It is not believed the island itself played a key role during the Revolution, but the immediate area, especially the larger island to the south- storied Valcour Island, was to play a role the significance of which is still being discovered to this day.

In late August, early September, an American invasion force under General Richard Montgomery moved north up the lake. A parallel force set out through the wilderness of Maine. Their intention was to take the key British outposts of Montreal and Quebec. As it had so many times previously, the island of St. Michel witnessed hundreds of bateaux laden with men and munitions en route to war.

In April 1776, a boat carrying Benjamin Franklin, Samuel Chase and Charles Carroll passed the island en route to Montreal to negotiate with the Canadians. Their efforts fail, along with the invasion itself. By June of 1776 the plucky American invasion force was engaged in a miserable retreat south up the lake from Canada. Hundreds of bateaux, laden with the ragged, sick and wounded remnants of Montgomery's army retreated towards the forts at Crown Point and Ticonderoga. It was a time of unspeakable misery for the Americans on the lake. They left behind hundreds of their colleagues in unmarked graves at places such as Isle aux Noix and Isle aux Tetes and Isle la Motte. It is possible some were left behind at Isle St. Michel. We do not know for sure... possibly another of Crab Island's secrets. With their sorrowful journey south, goes any hope of uniting North America as one against British rule.

This aerial view shows the scene of the Battle of Valcour in the foreground, Crab Island and Cumberland Head just to the north. (Roger and Doug Harwood photo)

The summer of 1776 was spent fortifying the important outposts at Crown Point and Ticonderoga. Both sides were engaged in constructing fleets with which each hoped to gain control of the lake. These fleets would clash in an epic battle just south of Crab Island at Valcour.

The morning of October 11, 1776 saw an enormous British flotilla round Cumberland Head, pass Crab Island and continue to the south. A truly impressive force, it consisted of approximately 30 major vessels, almost 700 picked seamen, together with a number of soldiers, artillerists and Indians in canoes. Their goal was to destroy the rebel fleet on Lake Champlain, take the vital American forts at Ticonderoga and Mt. Independence, and drive a wedge between the eastern and western parts of the Colony. Several days behind this naval force was an invading army, some 7,000 troops in almost 400 bateaux.

Awaiting them, hidden behind a large island just south of the Head, was a motley assortment of vessels-15 in all- hastily constructed of green timber shortly before at Skenesborough- the southernmost head of navigation on the lake. Formed in a line within a channel at most a half-mile wide, this ragged fleet awaited the mighty flotilla from the north. There were some 800 men aboard these vessels, described by their own commander as "a wretched, motley crew." Many had endured unimaginable hardships to serve aboard these ships, most were lacking in the most basic of provisions, and some had no shoes. All were hungry, tired and apprehensive.

The British fleet sailing south from Canada consisted of the *Inflexible*, a ship of 18 guns, two schooners- the *Maria* and the *Carleton*, fourteen and twelve guns, an enormous radeau bristling with heavy weapons, the *Thunderer*, and a large gondola- the *Royal (or Loyal) Convert*.

Together with 20 gunboats and another two dozen longboats, they sailed south past Cumberland Head on a brisk autumn breeze. On both sides of the lake, the hills blazed with the reds, yellows and oranges of a New England fall. Within a few hours, these same colors would light up the sky and reflect on the waters off Valcour Island- this time the source of the brilliant canvas would not be nature, but the horrifying killing machines of man.

Aboard the Flagship *Maria*, Captained by Thomas Pringle, was Sir Guy Carleton himself, British Governor of Canada. They had much intelligence on the ships the rebels were building on the lake and the British High Command had seen to it that naval superiority was achieved. They expected to meet their enemy in the vicinity of Crown Point, and with such overwhelming strength, it was believed they would easily reopen the vital lake corridor to His Majesty's army.

The Americans spotted the British first. Seeing the size of the oncoming fleet, General Waterbury had second thoughts about Benedict Arnold's plan to hole up in the protected lee of Valcour. Calling a hasty council of war, he entreated Arnold to leave the shelter of the island and meet the enemy in the broad lake, while attempting a retreat to relative security under the guns of Ticonderoga and Independence. Arnold would have nothing to do with it- he ordered the lines of battle tightened and told his commanders to prepare to fight.

It was some time after 10:00 that the British finally caught sight of the American vessels. By that time the brisk wind from the north had taken them too far south, past the island, and it was necessary to attempt to change direction- against the wind- back towards the west in order to engage the enemy. Arnold was determined the British come to him- he had sent out a couple of schooners and some gallies to entice his antagonists into the bay. The gunboats came into range first, and the engagement began in earnest about 11:00. Early on, things took a dramatic turn for the worst for the rebels. The *Royal Savage*, the largest vessel in the American fleet, ran hard aground on the rocky southwestern corner of the island. Already heavily damaged by some well-placed shots from the *Inflexible*, this was a loss the tiny American fleet could scarcely afford. Seeing her plight, several gunboats turned their fire on the helpless vessel while the crew abandoned her and fled into the woods. Not all escaped, however, since a boarding party from the *Loyal Convert* quickly came aside, and captured 20 of her sailors. Lt. Edward Longcroft then turned the *Savage's* guns against her own ships. This lasted only a short time before long the blazing fury of the nearby rebel fleet was turned onto the *Savage*, and the redcoats were forced to abandon her again. They would return again- this time to set the vessel afire.

For several hours a fierce battle ensued. As Arnold himself says:

> "...at, half past 11 the engagement, became General, & very warm...Some of the Enemies Ships & all their Gondolas, beat & rowed up within musquet Shott of us. they, Continued a Very hot fire with Round & Grape Shott..."[1] .

By 12:30 pm the *Carleton* and several gunboats had managed to get within musket shot of the American lines. The *Congress*, with Arnold aboard, took a terrific beating. By mid-afternoon, the *Washington* had been hulled in several places, her mast was gone and most of her sails were in shreds. On both shores a number of Indians had been landed, they kept up an incessant hail of musket fire upon the American vessels. Arnold continues:

"... the Congress & Washington have sufferd. greatly, the Latter Lost her first Lieut killed, & Capt & Master wounded, the New York lost all her officers except her captain. the Philada was hulled in so many Places that She Sank, About One hour after the engagemt was over, the whole, killed & wounded amounts to abt Sixty, the enemy, Landed a large Number of Indians On the Island & each Shore, who. keep an Incessant Fire On us, but did little Damage- the Enemy had to Appearance Upwards of One thousand Men in Batteaus, prepared for boarding. - We suffered much for want of Seamen & Gunners, I was obliged myself to Point Most of the Guns on board the Congress which I believe did good execution- the Congress received Seven Shott between Wind & Water, was hulled a doz times, had her Main Mast Wounded in Two places & her Yard in One, The Washington was hulled a Number of times, her Main Mast Shot thro. & must have a New One. both Vessells are very leaky & want repairing...."[2]

Despite their best efforts, the largest ships were unable to come into range and bring most of their guns to bear. The *Carleton*, commanded by Lt. James Dacres, put up a fierce fight and paid a heavy price. Half her crew were killed or wounded. Dacres himself was rendered unconscious and command passed to Midshipman Edward Pellew, only 19 years old. Pellew proceeded to distinguish himself by his bravery.

By late-afternoon, the *Thunderer* and *Maria* still had not taken an active role in the engagement. In the case of the *Thunderer*, this may be understandable. The huge ship simply may not have been able to come around. The *Maria's* lack of involvement was to cause some controversy. Aboard were the Capt. Thomas Pringle, the Commander of naval operations, and the Governor-General himself, Sir Guy Carleton. Later, after the battle was over, the officers of the ships that did engage formally accused Pringle of mismanagement, and there were some hints at allegations of cowardice.

The battle continued through the afternoon, only beginning to abate around 5:00 pm. Finally, the British gunboats began to pull back, though sporadic firing continued well into the early autumn darkness. The American rebels took stock- at least 60 killed and wounded, the *Congress* badly damaged, along with the *Washington* and *New York*. The *Royal Savage*, of course, was gone; and the *Philadelphia* was sinking fast. A British boarding party had returned to the *Savage* and set her afire. She burned well into the evening, when a gigantic explosion lit the sky- the magazine had been touched off by the flames. With the loss of this ship went all of Arnold's personal papers and most of his belongings.

Sometime before 7:00 pm, the commanders of each vessel assembled aboard the *Congress* for a Council of War. The British would sit and wait out the darkness, finishing off the rebel fleet with the coming of day. Somehow, the battered fleet needed to get away from the superior guns of their adversaries and reach relative safety at Crown Point. An unlikely and exceedingly daring plan was proposed- they would sneak around the waiting British fleet, rowing close to the shore, oars muffled, lanterns out until they attained the broad lake, where they could "make a run" for the south.

The *Trumbull*, Col. Wigglesworth commanding, went first. He was followed by the *Enterprise* and the *Lee*, then each of the gondolas. The *Washington*, and finally the *Congress*, brought up the rear. A single, shuttered lantern in the stern of each ship was meant to be followed by each succeeding vessel. Incredibly, the entire group of ships made it past the waiting British fleet. Some say the British were distracted by the fire and explosions on the south shore of the island. Certainly, the tasks of caring for the wounded and preparing for the finale to occur the next morning was daunting. Yet, it is amazing that all of the American ships were able to slip by each of the British vessels unnoticed. Arnold described the escape with rather atypical modesty:

"... On Consulting with Genl Waterbury & Colonel Wiggilsworth, it was thought prudent to Retire to Crown Point, every Vessells Ammunition being Nearly three fourths spent. & the Enemies greatly Superior to us in Ships & Men - at. 7 oClock Colonel Wiggilsworth in the Trumbull got under Way, the Gondolas and Small Vessells followed & the Congress & Washington brought up the Rear. the Enemy did not, attempt to molest us, most of the fleet is this minute came to An Anchor, the Wind is small to the So ward, the, Enemies fleet is Under way to Leward & beating up.- as soon as our Leakes are Stoped, the whole fleet will, made the utmost Dispatch to Crown Point, where I beg you will Send Ammunition & your further Orders for us. - On the whole I think we have had a Very fortunate escape..."[3]

Governor Carleton, however; admitted to being impressed with the escape:

"... We then Anchored in a line opposite the Rebels within the distance of Cannon shot, expecting in the morning to be able to engage them with our whole fleet, but, to our great mortification we perceived at day break, that they had found means to escape us unobserved by any of our guard boats or cruizers, thus an opportunity of destroying the whole rebel naval force, at one stroke, was lost, first by an impossibility of bringing all our vessels to action, and afterwards by the great diligence used by the enemy in getting away from us..."[4]

By daybreak, Arnold's wounded and motley fleet had reached Schuyler's Island, some nine miles from Valcour. Here they took the time to again take stock by the light of day. It was also here that Arnold wrote General Gates, as we have seen; his letter shares the details of the battle. In a footnote to the letter he pleads for a dozen bateau to help tow the damaged vessels back to Crown Point. He knew that soon a reckoning would occur. Their enemy would pursue them... and with the renewed zeal of an angry and embarrassed antagonist.

Arnold found two more of his vessels could not continue the flight south. These ships-gondolas- were sunk in the waters off Schuyler's Island.

Meanwhile, the British had discovered to their horror that the rebel fleet had escaped. An enraged General Carleton ordered the pursuit. The battle would continue into a second phase- the "running battle."

After taking care of a crisis with the *Thunderer* (the huge ship had lost her lee boards and was listing so much she was taking on water) the fleet set out to catch up with the rebels. Orders were given to the ground troops to follow in the rear, and thanks to a freshening wind, good time was made heading up the lake. Just North of Split Rock, the first of the ships were overtaken. In a desperate move, the hybrid Cutter *Lee* was run into a bay on the eastern shore where she was taken as a prize. The already battered *Washington* took several more broadsides, and then she was forced to strike her colors. General Waterbury was taken captive along with her crew. The *Jersey* is believed to have capitulated at Split Rock also (although some believe she was scuttled at Schuyler's Island.) The plucky *Congress*, with a determined Benedict Arnold aboard, refused to give up. This time it was the British ships, with all their massive firepower, that were coming to bear upon the American vessels- the gunboats were still lagging behind, and played a lesser role in this second phase of the battle.

Arnold was desperate- he saw that they wouldn't be able to reach Crown Point. He knew whatever ships were captured would be used again- the very ships he had worked so hard to see built at Skenesborough would be used against him in the future. He decided to run his remaining vessels aground, burn them, and make a desperate run across land to Ticonderoga.

The vicinity of Crab Island was the scene of a truly pivotal exchange- one that played a crucial war in the history of the Revolution. The British won what was to prove to be a rather hollow victory at Valcour, the battle was carried south past Split Rock to Ferris's Bay. Seeing the mighty fortifications at Ticonderoga and Mt. Independence, Carleton turned his fleet around and returned to Canada for the winter. Several months later another mighty armada would travel south past Crab Island.

On June 13, 1777, an awesome military force left St. Johns on the Richelieu for an expedition up Lake Champlain. Their objective was nothing less than the splitting of New England from the rest of the colonies. By June 16th, Burgoyne's mighty army was encamped just north of Crab Island on the large peninsula known as Cumberland Head. The massive force consisted of

"The Ship Royal George, 24 Guns, *Ship Inflexible*, 20 Guns, *Brigg Washington*, 16, *Schooner* Maria, 14, *Schooner* Carlton, 12, *Cutter* Lee, 10. *Radeau*, now carrying 18, *Gondolas* Loyal

Convert, 9, *Gondolas Jersey*, 7, and 24 Gun Boats, Mann'd and armed as last year with Brass Artillery "‡

Accompanying these large vessels were hundreds of bateaux and long-boats carrying thousands of troops.

We know that Burgoyne's mighty force sailed south to ultimate defeat at Saratoga. With this loss came the beginning of the end for His Majesty's forces in New England. Ultimately, the American rebels emerged victorious, and events upon Lake Champlain and Lake George were to prove key to the resolution of this latest contest in North America.

A new nation was the result.

Notes:

[1]: Brigadier General Benedict Arnold to Major General Horatio Gates; Schuyler Island Octr 12. 1776 Gates Papers, Box 4, NYHS. Naval Documents of the American Revolution, Vol. 6. Naval History Division, Dept. of the Navy. Washington: 1972

[2]: Ibid.

[3]: Ibid.

[4]: Governor Sir Guy Carleton to Lieutenant General John Burgoyne; On Board the Maria off Isle Valcour October [October 12 to October 15] Guy Carleton Letter Book, Haldimand Papers- Naval Documents of the American Revolution, Vol. 6. Naval History Division, Dept. of the Navy. Washington: 1972

‡ James Hadden. Hadden's Journal and Orderly Books: A Journal Kept in Canada and Upon Burgoyne's Campaign in 1776 and 1777, by Lieut. James M. Hadden, Roy. Art. Edited by Horatio Rogers. (Albany: Joel Munsell's Sons, 1884)

VI. War of 1812- The Battle of Plattsburgh: The Military Hospital, Battery and Burial Ground

Once again the winds of war would blow south over the crucial Richelieu River/Lake Champlain corridor. The region played a key role in what has been referred to as America's second war of independence. Repeated American incursions into Canada had proven disastrous and now the British had decided to bring the war into the United States. In September 1814 the British invasion began, a massive force surged south over land and water. They would meet their foes at a place named Plattsburgh.

The Battle at the bridge over the Saranac River, Battle of Plattsburgh

The British army and navy were not the only enemies the young American military had to deal with. Disease and desertion were formidable foes for both sides. A pressing need to deal with both brought tiny Crab Island to the attention of the American forces here. Army surgeon James Mann tells us much about the situation in Plattsburgh at the time:

> "While the army under the command of General IZARD retrograded from Champlain to Plattsburgh, the last week in August, and continued its route to Sackett's Harbour, the sick of that division were left at Plattsburgh, under my direction, with only one assistant capable of duty. Upon the 1st of September, the returns of the sick, including the regimental and hospitals reports, were 921.
>
> The British army followed General IZARD'S retrograde march. Upon the 6th of September, Plattsburgh was invested with an army of between 14 and 15,000 men; when the sick unable to perform garrison duty were ordered to be transported to Crab Island, about two miles from

the fortifications; as they could not be covered within the lines of defence. At this time the general hospital reports alone counted 720 men."[1]

Plattsburgh was the scene of feverish activity as the British onslaught pushed south from the border. The residents of the town had fled; General Alexander Macomb decided to use the natural barrier of the Saranac River as an aid in his defense against the invaders. A series of fortifications were hastily erected on the south bank of the river, time was of the essence- those unable to work were transported to Crab Island.

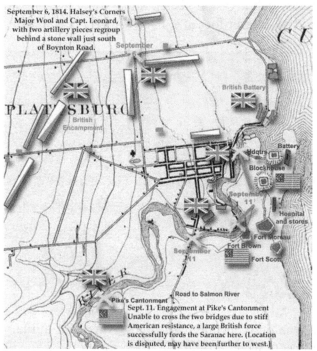

On September 3, Dr. Mann wrote his superiors in an earnest plea for assistance:

"The sick and convalescents have been ordered to Burlington Vermont; but for want of transportation, are removing to Crabb Island, two miles and a half from the fortifications at Plattsburgh. Such of the convalescents as can perform garrison duty are ordered into the forts. More than five hundred have already arrived at Crabb Island, a barren uninhabited spot. Hospital tents to cover them have been furnished. Doctor PURCELL is now my only assistant, and he is sick, RUSSELL is ordered into one of the forts..."[2]

By September 10, hundreds had been evacuated south to the hospital at Burlington. However, the engagements at Culver Hill and Halsey's Corners resulted in another 40 or so wounded being shipped to the tents on the island. Mann wrote of the distressing situation on the island. His troubles were nothing compared to what was in store the next morning.

September 11th dawned and two mighty navies clashed just north of Crab Island in Cumberland Bay. The deafening roar of cannon fire was accompanied by clouds of smoke blocking the view of the fearsome conflict. The following account of the battle is from **"The Battle of Plattsburgh- What Historians Say About It"**, published in 1914 at the Centenary of the battle:

This dramatic image of Commodore Macdonough on the Saratoga was taken from "The Battle of Plattsburgh- What Historians Say About it", published in 1914.

"The morning of September 11th opened with a light breeze from the northwest. Downie's fleet weighed anchor at daylight, and came up the lake with the wind nearly aft, the booms of the two sloops, swinging out to starboard. At half past seven, the people in the ships could see their adversaries' upper sails across the narrow strip of land ending in Cumberland Head, before the British doubled the latter. Captain Downie hove to with his four large vessels, when he had fairly opened the bay, and waited for his galleys to overtake him. Then his four vessels filled on the starboard tack and headed for the American line, going abreast, the *Chub* to the north, heading well to windward of the *Eagle*, for whose bows the *Linnet* was headed, while the *Confiance* was to be laid athwart the hawser of the *Saratoga*; the *Finch* was to leeward with the twelve gunboats, and was to engage the rear of the American line.

As the English squadron stood bravely in, young Macdonough, who feared his foes not at all, but his God a great deal, knelt for a moment, with his officers on the quarter-deck; and then ensued a few minutes of perfect quiet, the men waiting with grim expectancy for the opening of the fight. The *Eagle* spoke first with her long 18's, but to no effect, for the shot fell short. Then, as the *Linnet* passed the *Saratoga*, she fired her broadside of long 12's, but her shot also fell short, except one that struck a hencoop that happened to be aboard the *Saratoga*. There was a gamecock inside, and, instead of being frightened at his sudden release, he jumped up on a gun-slide, clapped his wings, and crowed lustily. The men laughed and cheered, and immediately afterward Macdonough himself fired the first shot from one of the long guns. The 24-pound ball struck the *Confiance* near the hawse-hole and ranged the length of her deck, killing and wounding several men. All the American long guns now opened and were replied to by the British galleys.

The *Confiance* stood steadily on without replying. But she was baffled by shifting winds, and was soon so cut up, having both her port bow-anchors shot away, and suffering much loss, that she was obliged to port her helm and come to while still nearly a quarter of a mile distant from the *Saratoga*. Captain Downie came to anchor in grand style, securing everything carefully before he fired a gun, and then opening with a terribly destructive broadside. The *Chub* and *Linnet* stood further in, and anchored forward the *Eagle's* beam. Meanwhile the *Finch* got abreast of the *Ticonderoga*, under her sweeps, supported by the gun boats. The main fighting was thus to take place between the vans, where the *Eagle*, *Saratoga*, and six, or seven gun boats were engaged with the *Chub*, *Linnet*, *Confiance*, and two or three gun boats; while in the rear, the *Ticonderoga*, the *Preble*, and the other American galleys engaged the *Finch* and the remaining nine or ten English galleys. The battle at the foot of the line was fought on the part of the Americans to prevent their flank being turned, and on the part of the British to effect that object. At first the fighting was at long range, but gradually the British galleys closed up, firing very well. The American galleys at this end of the line were chiefly the small ones, armed with one 12-pounder apiece, and they by degrees drew back, before the heavy fire of their opponents. About an hour after the discharge of the first gun had been fired; the *Finch* closed up toward the *Ticonderoga*, and was completely crippled by a couple of broadsides from the latter. She drifted helplessly down the line and grounded near Crab Island; some of the convalescent patients manned the six-pounder and fired a shot or two at her, when she struck, nearly half of her crew being killed or wounded.

About the same time the British gunboats forced the *Preble* out of line, whereupon she cut her cable and drifted inshore out of the fight. Two or three of the British gunboats, had already been sufficiently damaged by some of the shot from the *Ticonderoga's* long guns to make them wary; and the contest at this part narrowed down to one between the American schooner and the remaining British gunboats who combined to make a most determined attack upon her. So hastily had the squadron been fitted out that many of the matches for her guns were at the last moment found to be defective. The Captain of one of the divisions was a midshipman, but 16 years old, Hiram Paulding. When he found the matches to be bad he fired the guns of his section by having pistols flashed at them, and continued this through the whole fight. The *Ticonderoga's* commander, Lieutenant Cassin, fought his schooner most nobly. He kept walking the taffrail amidst showers of musketry and grape, coolly watching the movements of the galleys and directing the guns to be loaded with canister and bags of bullets when the enemy tried to board. The British galleys were handled with determined gallantry, under the command of Lieutenant Bell. Had they driven off the *Ticonderoga* they would have won the day for their side, and they pushed up till they were not a boathook's length distant, to try to carry her by boarding; but every attempt was repulsed and they were forced to draw off, some of them so crippled by the slaughter they had suffered they could hardly man the oars.

Meanwhile, the fighting at the head of the line had been even fiercer. The first broadside of the *Confiance*, fired from 16 long 24's, double-shotted, coolly sighted in smooth water, at point blank range, produced the most terrible effect on the *Saratoga*. Her hull shivered all over with the shock, and when the crash subsided nearly half her people were seen stretched on deck, for many had been knocked down, who were not seriously hurt. Among the slain were her first lieutenant, Peter Gamble; he was kneeling down to sight the bow-gun, when a shot entered the port, split the quoin, and drove a portion of it against this side, killing him without breaking the skin. The survivors carried on the fight with undiminished energy. Macdonough himself worked like a common sailor, in pointing and handling a favorite gun. While bending over to sight it, a round shot cut in two the spanker boom which fell on his head and struck him senseless for two or three minutes; he then leaped to his feet and continued as before, when a shot took off the head of the captain of the gun crew and drove it in his face with such a force as to knock him to the other side of the deck, but after the first broadside not so much injury was done; the guns of the *Confiance* had been leveled to point blank range, and the quoins were loosened by the success of discharges they were not properly replaced, so that her broadside kept going higher and higher, and doing less and less damage.

Very shortly after the beginning of the action her gallant captain was slain. He was standing behind one of the long guns, when a shot from the *Saratoga* struck it, and threw it completely off the carriage against his right groin killing him almost instantly. His skin was not broken; a black mark about the size of a small plate was the only visible injury. His watch was found flattened, with its hands pointing the very second at which he received the fatal blow.

As the contest went on the fire gradually decreased in weight, the guns being disabled. The inexperience of both crews partly caused this. The American sailors overloaded their carronades so as to very much destroy the effect of the fire; when the officers became disabled, the men would cram the guns with shot till the last projected from the muzzle; of course, this lessened the execution, and also gradually crippled the guns. On board the Confiance the confusion was even worse; after the battle the charges of the guns were drawn, and on the side she had fought one was found with a canvas bag containing two round of shot rammed home and wadded without any powder; another with two cartridges and no shot; and a third with a wad below the cartridge.

At the extreme head of the line the advantage had been with the British. The *Chub* and *Linnet* had begun a brisk engagement with the *Eagle* and American gunboats. In a sort time the *Chub* had her cable, bow-sprit and main-boom shot away, drifted within the American lines, and was taken possession of by one of the *Saratoga's* midshipman. The *Linnet* paid no attention to the American gunboats, directing her whole fire against the *Eagle*, and the latter was, in addition, exposed to part of the fire of the *Confiance*. After keeping up a heavy fire for a long time here springs were shot away, and she came up into the wind, hanging so that she could not return a shot to the well directed broadsides of the *Linnet*. Henley accordingly cut his cable, started home his top-sails, ran down, and anchored by the stern between and inshore of the *Confiance* and *Ticonderoga*, form which position he opened on the *Confiance*. The *Linnet* now directed her attention to the American gunboats, which at the end of the line were very well fought, but she soon drove them off, and then sprung her broadside so as to rake the *Saratoga* on her bows.

Macdonough by this time had his hands full, and his fire was slackening; he was bearing the whole brunt of the action, with the frigate on his beam and the brig raking him. Twice had his ship been set on fire by the hot shot of the *Confiance*; one by one his long guns were disabled by shot, and his carronades were either treated the same way or else rendered useless by excessive overcharging. Finally but a single carronade was left in the starboard batteries and on manning it the naval-bolt broke, the gun flew off the carriage and fell down the main hatch, leaving the Commodore without a single gun to oppose to the few the *Confiance* still presented. The battle would have been lost had not Macdonough's foresight provided the means of retrieving it. The anchor suspended astern of the *Saratoga* was let go, and the men hauled in on the hawser that led to the starboard quarter, bringing the ship's stern up over the kedge. The ship now rode by the kedge and by a line that had been bent to a bight in the stern cable, and she was raked badly by the accurate fire of the *Linnet*. By rousing on the line the ship was at length got so far round that the aftermost gun of the port broadside bore on the *Confiance*. The men had been sent forward to keep as much out of harm's way as possible, and now some were at once called back to man the piece, which then opened with effect. The next gun was treated in the same manner; but the ship now hung and would go no further round. The hawser leading from the port quarter was then got forward under the bows and passed aft to the starboard quarter, and a minute afterward the ship's whole port battery opened with fatal effect. The *Confiance* meanwhile had also attempted to round. Her springs, like those of the *Linnet*, were on the starboard side, and so of course, could not be shot away as the *Eagle's* were; but, as she had nothing but springs to rely on, her efforts did little but beyond forcing her forward and she hung with her head to the wind. She had lost over half her crew, most of her guns on the engaged side were dismounted, and her stout masts had been splintered till they looked like bundles of matches her sails had been torn to rags, and she was forced to strike about two hours after she had fired the first broadside. Without pausing a minute the *Saratoga* again hauled on her starboard hawser till her broadside was sprung to bear on the *Linnet*, and the ship and brig began a brisk fight, which the *Eagle*, from her position could take no part in, while the *Ticonderoga* was just finishing up the British galleys. The shattered and disabled state of the *Linnet's* masts, sails, and yards precluded the most distant hope of Captain Pring's effecting his escape by cutting his cable, but he kept up a most gallant fight with his greatly superior foe, in hopes that some of the gunboats would come and tow him off, and dispatched a lieutenant to the *Confiance* to ascertain her state. The lieutenant returned with news of Captain Downie's death while the British gunboats had been driven half a mile off; and, after having maintained the fight single-handed for fifteen minutes, until the number of shots between wind and water, the water had risen a foot above her lower deck, the plucky little brig hauled down her colors, and the fight ended. A little over two hours and a half after the first gun had been fired not one of the larger vessels had a mast that would bear canvas, and the prizes were in a sinking condition. The British galley's drifted to leeward, none with their colors up, but as the *Saratoga's* boarding-official passed along the deck of the *Confiance* he accidentally ran against a lock spring on one of her starboard guns, and it went off. This was apparently understood as a signal by the galleys, and they moved slowly off, pulling but a very few sweeps, and not one of them hoisting an ensign. On both sides the ships had been cut up in a most extraordinary manner; the *Saratoga* had 55 shot holes in her hull, and the *Confiance* 105 in hers, and the *Eagle* and *Linnet* suffered in proportion. The number killed and wounded cannot be exactly stated; it was probably about 200 on the American side and over 300 on the British..." [3]

Midway through the action, the invalid crew manning a two-gun battery on the northeast shore was stunned to find the British sloop *Finch* bearing down upon the island. Soon, the vessel was hopelessly aground upon the reef. Gallant efforts were made to lighten the ship so that it might return to the fight, to no avail. Four 18-pounder carronades were tossed overboard, nothing helped. The battery on Crab opened up on the stranded ship with round and grape shot. The *Finch* returned fire. According to her Captain, William Hicks, the crew of the *Finch* "had the pleasure of killing or wounding every man at the guns on shore and silence them."[4] The contingent at Crab Island contributed some of their own ranks to the services of the surgeons.

When the terrible battle was over, the hospital on the island received the wounded of both fleets. Dreadful scenes of death and destruction were everywhere as boat after boat arrived with their appalling cargo. The British flagship *Confiance* alone contributed some 83 wounded, 41 of them listed as "dangerously or seriously wounded." This, on top of 40 killed outright on the ship during the battle.[5] Along with the British dead and wounded came the American combatants. Mortal enemies who just hours before had fought furiously with each other now lay side by side in rows in the hospital tents. Outside the tents, rows upon rows of British and American warriors, many not much older than children, together awaited the burial that must come soon.

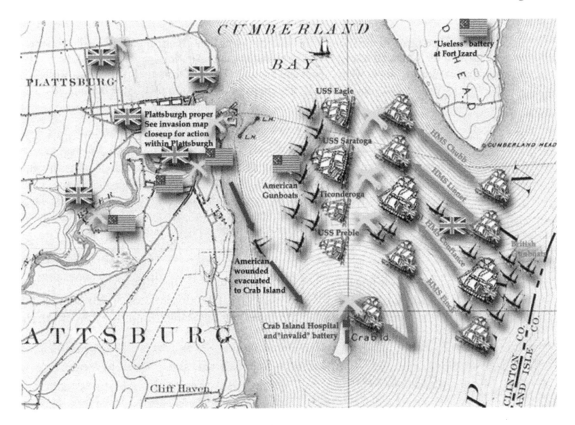

Other than Dr. James Mann's account of the situation on Crab Island, only one other piece has become known detailing the situation on Crab Island immediately following the battle. Printed in the Plattsburgh Republican of September 22, 1877 it records the recollections of Simeon Doty of Chazy.

"...Mr. Doty was a member of Captain Hazen's company on Grand Isle and was on that island the day the battle was fought, the troops there being unable to get across to help their comrades. He crossed the next day (Monday, Sept. 12), however, with Capt. Hazen and others in a small boat, and went on board several of the vessels which had been in the battle; and among others the one which Commodore Downie was killed [Confiance], and whose body he saw wrapped up below. He also saw Commodore Macdonough pacing the deck of his own vessel with his colored servant near him and afterwards went ashore on Crab Island where the dead were being taken by jolly boats and buried, the wounded being already there.

The boats landed on the north end of the island next to Cumberland Head and the hospital tents were located just south of the landing in the bushes. These tents were built of boards and canvass and were ranged from east to west. A sentry who wore a red coat and who, Mr. Doty thinks, was a British prisoner, was pacing up and down between the tents and keeping guard. He saw many of the bodies were terribly mutilated as they were brought ashore- in some cases only dismembered limbs and other portions having been found, and he recollects well of seeing human entrails and other parts which, as he supposes, had been thrown overboard from the vessels, floating up to the shore at the landing. Inside tents the scene was a terrible one. Shrieks from the wounded soldiers who were undergoing operations at the hands of the surgeons rent the air; others were crying and begging for relief from their sufferings, while men were constantly carrying out the dead on rude biers made of poles to the burial yard south of the hospital tents.

Here our informant saw trenches dug, ranging from north to south into which the bodies were placed. Some of them were rolled up in blankets and other had only their ordinary clothing on; their heads were placed to the west and their faces downward. The Americans and British were buried indiscriminately together, probably to the number of at least one hundred, and there they lie today, their graves unmarked, save by a number of long rude mounds indicating the site of the ditches in which they were huddled sixty-three years ago. A visit to Crab Island last Saturday disclosed this to us, and also a few decayed scraps of boards which mark the spot where the hospital tents stood." [6]

Some time later Caleb Nichols, the owner of the island at the time of its use by the American forces, submitted a bill to the government. This document, on display at the Clinton County Historical Museum in Plattsburgh, is transcribed here with their permission.

Notes:

*Caleb Nichols bill transcribed from a photocopy of the original in the collections of the Clinton County Historical Museum in Plattsburgh, NY.

[1] James Mann, "MEDICAL SKETCHES OF THE CAMPAIGNS OF 1812, 13, 14. TO WHICH ARE ADDED, SURGICAL CASES; OBSERVATIONS ON MILITARY HOSPITALS; AND FLYING HOSPITALS ATTACHED TO A MOVING ARMY." 1816 (DEDHAM: Printed by H. Mann and Co.)
[Note: Mann's account is discussed and excerpted here- http://www.historiclakes.org/Plattsburg/mann.htm.]

[2] Ibid.

[3] New York State Commission, Plattsburg Centenary. 1914. The Battle of Plattsburgh- What Historians Say About It. (Albany, NY: J. B. Lyon Company.)13-20

[4] The Court martial of Captain Daniel Pring and the Officers and Men Employed in the Squadron on Lake Champlain. August 18-21, 1815 on Board H.M.S *Gladiator* in Portsmouth Harbor. Public Records Office, Kew Gardens, London. Courtesy of James T. Hays and Addie Shields, Clinton County Historian.

[5] Ibid.

[6] Plattsburgh Republican: Plattsburgh, NY. Sept. 22, 187

The Caleb Nichols bill*

The United States

To C. Nichols, Dr.

For rent of and damages done to Crab Island by Commodore Macdonough's Fleet before the 20th October 1814.

1st. For 50 Cords of Timber taken from or used on the island	50.00
2. For 10 Sticks of Timber for use of the Fleet	5.00

3. For building and occupying on the Island, one Hospital, one Store House and one House, one Kitchen and several Necessaries for the uses of Surgeons and Sick of the Fleet, by which, besides the Rent of the Island, it being proper for Naval purposes, on account of the Size of the Island and its Situation in the Lake to prevent desertion. The following damages were sustained.

1st. Three acres of Meadow were so frequently run over by the Sick and dug up to get worms to fish with as to be destroyed so that it could not be mowed this year.	50.00
2. Occupying four acres of Garden or possessing them in Such Manner as to render them useless and for want of improvement to permit them to grow up to Canada thistles.	100.00
3. A Cow running over the whole for a long time.	10.00
4. Burying 150 men on the Island.	150.00
5. Taking down a log house to use about building the Hospital, Store and houses	50.00

Besides the above damages the Rent of the Island for Naval purposes, rating the rent at the rate the army has paid for land which it used for Military purposes.	200.00
	615.00

The 32-pounder Carronade that killed Captain Downie aboard the Confiance early in the battle. The muzzle still bears the indentation from the ball that struck the gun forcing it off its carriage and back onto Downie. These photos were taken by Roger Harwood at Macdonough Hall in Annapolis, Maryland.

HMS Confiance's huge anchor has been recovered from Cumberland Bay and is now displayed in Plattsburgh's City Hall. The large, wooden crosspieces have been removed and are shown in the photo at right. Photos by the author.

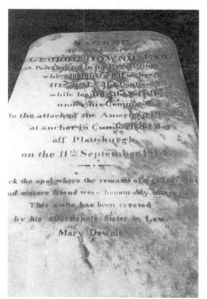

Left and above: The grave of Captain George Downie at Plattsburgh's Riverside Cemetery. The officers killed in the battle were interred here, side by side with their American antagonists. The enlisted men were buried together in a mass grave on Crab Island. The gravesite is unmarked to this day. Photos by the author.

VII. Caretakers of the Island: 1814-1908

Care·tak·er (ker′tāk′ər) *n.* ...2. a person temporarily carrying out the duties as of an office.[1]

So reads Webster's second definition of caretaker. Crab Island has had many such caretakers, individuals who have for one reason or another stepped in to temporarily carry out "the duties..." Their reasons have been many and varied. One was a caretaker in the most common, typical sense. Others, however, stepped in to do a job that they felt needed to be done, usually with no thought or consideration of recompense. They have made a difference on tiny Crab Island.

We do not know if Caleb Nichols ever submitted his bill to the government. We do know that the island needed some work after the US military left the island in 1814. We also know that before the battle, the island had at least one building on it and that it was actively farmed. Moreover, we know that the US military left behind something very special on this island- the gravesite of at least 150 men.

Crab Island is about 40 acres in size. Nichols' bill tells us that three acres were meadow (and were mowed); another four acres had been a garden before the island was taken over by the military. Had the rest been cleared? Probably not, the army was also billed for some "50 Cords of wood" and another "10 sticks of Timber for the use of the Fleet" so there was at least something of a woodlot.

We can assume the location of the graves was ignored right from the beginning. Plattsburg, like all the surrounding towns and cities, was anxious to put the war behind them and get down to the important business of promoting growth and prosperity. Some five years passed. Finally, in 1819, we get some idea of what sort of stewardship the island and its military cemetery had received. Noted writer Benjamin Silliman, traveling from St. Johns to Burlington aboard the steamboat Congress made this graphic and haunting observation as he passed Crab Island:

> "We passed close to the small island, called Crab-Island, to which the dead and wounded of both fleets were carried, and which was the common grave of hundreds of friends and foes. The particular details of the scenes of horror which attended and succeeded the battle--of the shocking mutilations of the human form, in every imaginable mode and degree, and of the appalling display on the beach, of so many bodies, dead and wounded, preparatory to their conveyance either to the hospital or the grave, I shall, for obvious reason, omit. *Even now, their bones, slightly buried on a rocky island, are partly exposed to view, or being occasionally turned up by the roots of trees, blown down by the wind, shock the beholder, and*

their buttons, and other parts of their clothes, (for the military dresses in which they were slain, were also their winding sheets,) are often seen above the ground. Long may it be, e'er the waters of this now peaceful lake are again crimsoned with human blood." [2] (Italics added).

It is possible Silliman may have been using a bit of artistic license here. Regardless of whether he saw these things or was told of them, it seems obvious there is an element of truth here.

The island's owner must have simply ignored the gravesite, shockingly so, it would seem. It would appear the island was not farmed again. Was it inhabited? Did anyone move back onto the island? It does not seem so. One can only imagine what it would have been like to live on a tiny island, knowing that such a place was just beyond the meadows and gardens of the homestead. We can assume these early owners did nothing to honor the dead buried under the shallow layer of soil on the island.

American and British officers are buried together in Plattsburgh, New York's Riverside Cemetery. The large, rectangular stone marks that of Capt. George Downie, commander of HMS Confiance. Photo by the author.

It was 1843 before the officer's graves in Riverside Cemetery received headstones. A group called the Clinton County Military Association collected public donations to purchase tombstones for the graves. Nothing was done to mark the mass grave on the island.[3]

Caleb Nichols died in 1858; the island was inherited by his brother's children. In 1867 it was purchased by William Mooers and Smith Weed for $1500. Finally; the island was getting public attention. Years of newspaper editorials clamored for "something to be done about the graves." In 1891, the partners sold the island to the US government for a mere $500. Ostensibly, the government was going to do something with the island.

On January 30, 1895 Capt. George E. Pond, Asst. Quartermaster at Plattsburgh Barracks, wrote the Quartermaster General in Washington "relative to locating the graves and erecting a monument to the memory of Soldiers and Sailors of the War of 1812, buried on Crab Island...there were buried at one time 136 bodies, and from the fact of the island having been a general hospital, not only for the desperately wounded men of the naval engagement, but also for the sick and wounded of the land forces, there must have been a great many more there buried of whom no record exists...It has not been occupied since the war of 1812 and is now thickly grown with timber and underbrush. There are a number of long, low, mounds on the island, supposed to be the graves of these man, though nothing exact is known about them. I propose to open those mounds in the Spring and to determine and mark the graves." [4]

We do not know if these mounds were ever "opened" by the army. We do know the army eventually followed up on Pond's recommendation "to honor the memories of these brave men who gave their lives in their country's service..." Pond requested that "a special appropriation be asked of Congress of $15,000. of which $10,000. be expended in suitably marking the graves and erecting a monument, and $5,000. in clearing up and parking the island and building a wharf to accommodate boats of moderate tonnage." [5]

Here was a request that the army erect a monument of some sort. The graves were going to be "suitably marked." It would be some time before the monument was erected. The island continued in the public eye, largely as a result of frequent mention in the Plattsburgh Republican, and through the efforts of the Catholic Summer School at Cliff Haven. This prompted what appears to be the last known sighting of the graves. In 1901, a group from the Catholic Summer School went to the island expressly to find the burial site. Evidently, the gravesite was found, as was reported in "Mosher's Magazine" of April 1902:

> "Their graves are still visible, but, sad to say, neglected and overrun by the tangled growth of nature... On August 18th a party led by Mr. Bixby made a

trip to the historic island especially for the purpose of inspecting the burial-place of the dead of the battle. It was with difficulty that they found the mounds marking the graves, overrun as these were with underbrush and surrounded by beds of poison ivy. Rev. Thomas McMillan, C.S.P., and Rev. T.A. Hendrick, of Rochester, N.Y., were most zealous in the search, and they were the first to find the main group of mounds."[6]

Here was an opportunity to mark the location. Sadly, it appears nothing was done at the time.

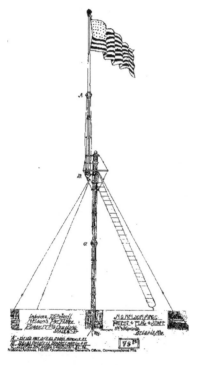

Soon, however, the island was receiving some of the attention it warranted. In 1903, a 100' iron flagstaff was erected on the south end of the island. The flagstaff was very distinctively designed, much like what one would find upon a naval vessel. One of several such masts in the country, it consisted of two main sections joined together about halfway up the mast. On Sept. 15, 1903, Captain Oliver Edwards, the Quartermaster at Plattsburgh Barracks, wrote the Adjutant that he "had received but one bid... for the foundation and erection of flag-staff... and that it was "four hundred and six dollars and fifty cents." This amount was over the original appropriation by some one hundred and forty-six dollars. Edwards then shared some interesting details about the character of the island when he wrote, "Mr. Wilcox (W.G. Wilcox of Plattsburgh, the sole bidder) states that he has made a careful estimate and does not care to undertake the work for any less than the amount bid. The erection of the flag-staff will be attended with considerable difficulty, owing to the distance from the main land, necessity of clearing ground to start with and the fact that in order to reach the depth required for the foundations it will be necessary to blast through solid rock, as the whole island is underlaid with a limestone rock at a depth of two or three feet below the surface."[7]

Wilcox's statement takes us back to the mystery of the graves. One wonders what sort of burial the soldiers received in 1814 if bedrock is found but "two or three feet below the surface?"

The flagstaff was erected on October 21 under the watchful eye of Colonel Adams of Plattsburgh Barracks. Crab Island finally had some sort of memorial commemorating its importance to the nation. The island was a military cemetery; at last the Stars and Stripes would fly over the island on important occasions.

It was another three years before Congress turned its attention to Crab Island again. When they did, however, the results were significant. On June 12, 1906 an appropriation was passed instructing the Army to "prepare the ground and suitably mark the graves of soldiers and sailors buried on Isle Saint Michel, commonly known as Crab Island (an appropriation of) the sum of $20,000, or such portion of as may be necessary." [8]

It appears work began by the end of the year. The island was cleared in many places ("parked" was the term used). A series of paths were cut in the woods, crisscrossing the entire island. By August of the following year, an attractive caretaker's cottage had been built about midway between the north and south ends of the island close to the western shore. It was not a large building, some 28' by 34', but contemporary photos show a lovely building with many windows and a small porch facing towards the lake.[9] Several outbuildings were erected, including a storehouse and wood and coal sheds. A large concrete pier was erected on the western shore, within view of the cottage. It would seem Crab Island was going to receive the attention it so richly deserved.

Crab Island outbuildings. Army records from 1914 list four outbuildings on the island; a wood and coal shed, stable, chicken-house, and a storehouse.

The caretaker's cottage at Crab Island. Erected August 1907

Sadly, however, it would appear this was not the case. On September 26, 1907 George Pond, now a General, again felt the need to write his superiors about the situation on Crab Island. His words are telling: "The efforts that have been made to park the island do not amount to anything and never will unless the assistance of the Bureau of Forestry is secured." He mentions the real need to clear trees and says he believes the bureau "would be very glad to tell... how the poison ivy, which is a veritable plague there, can be exterminated." There was a caretaker's house, but no one living in it. He mentions a need for a caretaker, and suggests that a retired soldier could take the job on, but they would need to be paid a salary. He stated "the only sensible and feasible thing to do is make this island a national cemetery." Interestingly enough, despite his earlier statement (January 1895) regarding a possible location of the graves, Pond now writes "the graves which have been neglected so long that it is not even known where they are buried." The Quartermaster General noted at the bottom of this letter, "it is desired that the matter be looked into by the proper branches and the QG furnished with a memorandum as to the plans..."[10]

Work of significance continued on the island in 1908. The paths in the woods were covered with a thin layer of stone, a windmill was built and most importantly, a monument was finally erected and a caretaker was hired. An impressive obelisk of Barre granite was erected just to the north of the caretaker's cottage. J.J. Fitzpatrick of Plattsburgh, the contractor, performed the work at a cost of $7,000. The obelisk, some 50' high, was supported by a granite base 23' wide. On each of the four faces of the monument was placed a bronze plate "suitably inscribed."

Above: The Crab Island Monument in 1909

These bronze plaques are no longer on the monument. In August, 2003 they were removed from the OPRHP's Peebles Island warehouse and put on display at the Clinton County Historical Association Museum in Plattsburgh.

The Crab Island Monument plaques have been restored and are now on display at the Clinton County Historical Association Museum in Plattsburgh.

Photos courtesy of Philip LaMarche.

Left: The Crab Island Monument plaques are displayed at the Clinton County Historical Association Museum on an exhibit designed and built by Roger Harwood to resemble the monument's obelisk. Roger Harwood photo

Monument Plaque Inscriptions

(East side)

NAVAL ENGAGEMENT
OFF
VALCOUR AND SCHUYLER ISLAND
LAKE CHAMPLAIN
OCT. 11th and 13th, 1776
AMERICAN LOSS
About 90.

(West side)

TO THE MEMORY
OF THE
OFFICERS, SOLDIERS and SAILORS
OF THE AMERICAN ARMY AND NAVY
WHO WERE KILLED
AT THE
BATTLE OF PLATTSBURGH, NEW YORK
SEPTEMBER 11, 1814
AND
BATTLE OF LAKE CHAMPLAIN,
SEPTEMBER 11, 1814
SECOND WAR WITH GREAT BRITAIN,
1812-1814-
AND
Naval Engagement
off
Valcour's and Schuyler's Islands,
Lake Champlain,
October 11 and 13, 1776.
Revolutionary War.

————

Erected by the War Department, U.S.A.
1908.

(North side)

BATTLE OF LAKE CHAMPLAIN
(NAVAL ENGAGEMENT)
SEPT. 11, 1814
AMERICAN SHIPS ENGAGED
Ship SARATOGA
Brig EAGLE
Schooner TICONDEROGA
Sloop PREBLE
GUNBOATS
BORER   CENTIPEDE
WILMER NETTLE
ALLEN VIPER
BURROWS LUDLOW
ALWYN BALLARD
AMERICAN LOSS
52 Killed 58 Wounded
Commodore Thomas Macdonough
Commanding the American Fleet

(South side)

BATTLE OF PLATTSBURGH
(LAND ENGAGEMENT)
SEPTEMBER 11, 1814
AMERICAN LOSS
37 KILLED, 65 WOUNDED, 20 MISSING
BRIGADIER GENERAL ALEXANDER MACOMB
COMMANDING THE AMERICAN ARMY

——

ON SEPTEMBER 11, 1814, THE BRITISH FORCES
MADE A COMBINED LAND AND NAVAL
ATTACK UPON THE AMERICAN ARMY
STATIONED AT PLATTSBURGH AND THE
AMERICAN SQUADRON IN PLATTSBURGH
BAY, LAKE CHAMPLAIN, BUT WERE
REPULSED, RESULTING IN ONE OF THE MOST
DECISIVE AMERICAN LAND AND NAVAL
VICTORIES OF THE WAR.

The other significant event of 1908 was the arrival of a caretaker and his family. Thomas P. Connolly, a retired post quartermaster sergeant, arrived to take up residence in the new cottage.

Notes:

[1] Webster's New World Dictionary: Second College Edition, Revised School Printing. 1985: New York: Simon and Schuster. 215

[2] Benjamin Silliman: Remarks Made on a Short Tour Between Hartford and Quebec in the Autumn of 1819. New Haven. CT. S. Converse, 1820. 375

[3] James G. Bailey: Crab Island-Walking Tour of Plattsburgh City Historian. Feb. 28, 1988

[4] George E. Pond letter: Office Constructing Quartermaster, Plattsburgh, N.Y. 79067-Q.M.G.O January 30, 1885.

[5] Ibid.

[6] Warren E. Mosher: "The Champlain Summer School- Crab Island A National Park" (Mosher's Magazine- April 1902, Vol. XX, No. 1) 208-209. Courtesy of Prof. Ray Patterson, Saint Michael's College.

[7] [Oliver?] Edwards letter: Office of the Quartermaster, Plattsburgh Barracks, N.Y. September 15, 1903.

[8] James G. Bailey, "THE FORGOTTEN GRAVES OF CRAB ISLAND" (The Antiquarian-Fall 1988, Allan Everest, Editor Clinton County Historical Association, Plattsburgh, NY) 14. Also republished with permission: America's Historic Lakes, <http://www.historiclakes.org/ccha/bailey1.htm > May 2001

[9] Quartermaster documents. Plattsburgh Barracks, N.Y. 48547: O.C.Q.M.E. January 28, 1911

[10] Quartermaster General- War Department letter. Washington. Statement dictated by General George E. Pond. September 26, 1907.

Ruins of the fireplace of the caretaker's cottage at Crab Island. Photo by the author.

VIII. Caretakers of the Island: The Connolly family 1908-1915

When Sergeant Thomas P. Connolly brought his family to live on Crab Island, much had been done to transform the small 40-acre military park. The monument had been erected; the island covered with a series of paths, the impressive naval style flagstaff now had someone to raise and lower the nation's standard daily.

Connolly was hired on October 1, 1908, at "$600 per annum, with quarters and fuel."[1] In 1909 the island was officially named MacDonough National Military Park. This park was the full-time residence of the Connolly family.

Connolly family outing: The pier at Crab Island. Photo courtesy of the Connolly family.

Thomas (b.1854) and Elizabeth (b.1865) Connolly had eight children. During the seven years they lived on Crab Island their descendants believe six of those children arrived upon this earth. It is likely that one of them was born on the island. The Connolly family has graciously provided some rare photos of the family at the time they lived there. The photos are old and yellowed; some are torn or have sections missing from them. And yet, they are truly wonderful images; they conjure up for this writer a phrase I have used before on this site- "ordinary people doing some rather extraordinary things."

We do not know much about what life was like for the family during those seven years. Nevertheless, we can imagine; and we can feel fairly comfortable our imaginings are not too far off the mark. Crab is at least a mile from the shore as the crow flies. Official military documents state it was 2.5 miles from the mainland- that must have been to the Plattsburgh Barracks dock or wharf. If Elizabeth did have six of her children while they lived on the island, one wonders what sort of anxiety they must have known during all the time she was with child. Imagine having to go to shore in that state to have the baby... or to have it on the tiny island?

The photos show a large family with several young children. We can be sure that those children came home regularly suffering from poison ivy- it was fittingly called "a plague" in the documents that have come to light. This writer can verify that the "plague" is still there. Despite the most strenuous efforts of the island's present-day "caretaker", (you will read about him later) the island is still covered with this deceptively harmless looking curse. I admit to a secret desire of my own that the vandals who have damaged the monument have experienced some sort of retribution from the island's most favored crop.

The island must have been a very lonely place. One can imagine the family sitting out on the cottage porch and seeing the lights of Plattsburgh in the distance. A mere mile or so of water can be quite a deterrent to the extension of warm hospitality. Winters on Lake Champlain can be especially difficult. The cold winds whip up the valley and chills to the bone anyone unfortunate enough to be outside. The valley receives less snowfall than the mountains on each side. Yet, the snow that falls is often seen coming to earth horizontally as it is whipped up by the prevailing winds causing near-zero visibility.

Did the family remain on the island during those seven winters? Again; we are not certain. It is possible the army expected the caretaker to remain there year round. Inspection reports complain of water facilities that did not work in the winter, necessitating the chopping of holes in the lake ice for water. It is likely it was this family that did the chopping. Connolly family oral tradition has the children being home-schooled on the island until the ice formed each year, and then traveling over the ice to reach school.

We will probably never really know much more about what life was like for this family during those years just prior to the First World War. Crab Island likes to keep its secrets to itself. In 1915, for reasons not yet known, the Connolly family left Crab Island for the last time.

Above: Sitting on the front steps of the caretaker's cottage- back row: Martin, Margaret, Thomas. Center row: Philip, Thomas P., Elizabeth, Marg. Front row: Isabel, Joseph, Catherine.

Left: Stairs of the caretaker's cottage- Martin, Mary, Tom, Elizabeth (Mother), and Philip Connolly.

Above, left: Caretaker Thomas P. Connolly outside the cottage. Photos courtesy of the Connolly family. Above, right: Swimming inside the pier at Crab Island- foreground: Margaret, Mary, Martin, Thomas. Background: Mother Connolly.

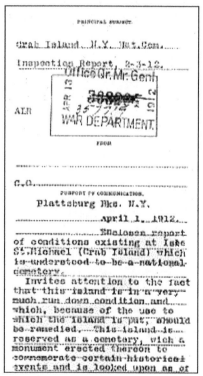

During the period when the Island had a full-time resident caretaker, we might reasonably assume the National Military Park was experiencing its best days. Unfortunately, this was not the case. Witness another document from Plattsburgh Barracks:

On February 3, 1912, 2nd Lt. Oliver Dickinson (Asst. Quartermaster) filed a "Crab Island, N.Y. Nat. Cem. Inspection Report."[2] The report states that the island still was not receiving the attention it required, despite having a full-time caretaker present.

Dickinson's remarked "this island is in a very much run down condition and which, because of the use to which the island is put, should be remedied." Among the specific problems noted were:

"The cottage is not sufficiently protected against the cold winter winds that sweep up and down the lake from north to south... the bathroom is useless because of no running water and this necessitates an outside privy, which is unsanitary and a menace to health."

"The windmill is so badly broken up that it is useless... water has to be dipped from the lake, a very evident hardship... particularly so in winter when a hole has to be chopped in the ice for this purpose."

"There was an abortive attempt to sink a well...about fifty yards from the cottage... carelessly covered over with old boards..."

"The walks around and across the island as represented on the map [see below] are mostly mythical, as the grass has grown up through the thin layer of small stones placed there some years ago to mark the walks, and these are poorly defined by the presence of these pebbles now."

"The cement topped pier is breaking up on top, whole sections having tilted up, and large cracks appearing, and in some spots the cement is all crumbled away."

"Outbuildings: These are an agglomeration of makeshift shacks and shanties...unsanitary shacks, located too close to the cottage and are altogether too small and entirely unsuited to their purpose..."

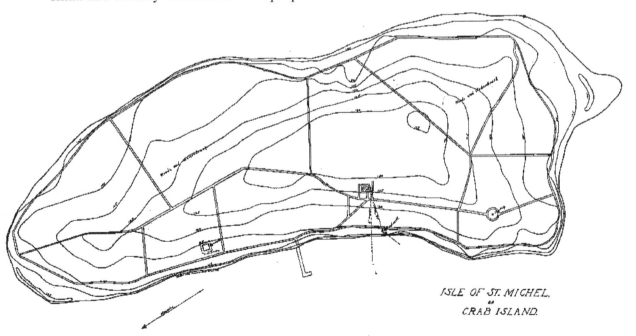

ISLE OF ST. MICHEL,
or
CRAB ISLAND.

Map, circa 1909 showing the improvements at Crab Island.

This, but 3 years after the island was designated a National Cemetery (at least that is the understanding the military had at Plattsburgh Barracks). It's true we don't know for sure why the Connolly family left Crab Island in 1915. In light of conditions at the time, however, it would seem we could make a fairly "educated" guess. Very little was done to improve the island. It would appear Thomas Connolly was having difficulty getting the material support he needed to properly maintain the park. In 1915 a water tank was finally installed in the attic of the cottage. It wasn't enough to keep the Connolly family there.

Sometime that year MacDonough National Military Park lost its first and only paid caretaker when the Connolly family left the island.

The Story Behind the Flagpole

There are not many photos in existence of the original flagstaff at Crab Island. Those that do exist are recent and show the once-impressive mast decrepit, rusting, and in very real danger of falling to the ground.

It was back in 1903 that Old Glory first waved from high atop the 100' mast at the southwestern end of the island.

The staff was erected in October 1903 by the Wilcox Company of Plattsburgh at a cost to the government of four hundred and six dollars and fifty cents. This may not

seem like much by today's standards, but in 1903 dollars, this was a princely sum. It was some one hundred and forty-six dollars over the original appropriation, the additional funds were insisted upon by the contractor due to the difficulty of the work.

Upon completion, the impressive staff towered above the oaks and white pines surrounding the clearing. The flag of the Republic was raised; at last, there was something to remind those passers-by on the lake and on the shore of the sacrifice of those buried on the island.

It was a fitting standard-bearer for Macdonough National Military Park.

Early military file photo of the Crab Island flagstaff.

Alas, even this proud symbol dedicated to the heroes of Plattsburgh would fall victim to ignorance and neglect. Within a few short years, Macdonough National Military Park was for all practical purposes abandoned. By 1915, there was no caretaker at the island to raise and lower the flag. We can not say for sure whether the nation's flag ever flew from the mast after 1915. For the most part, except for a brief flurry of activity in the mid-1950's [covered elsewhere in this publication] the island was left to revert back to nature.

Finally, in July 1996 the inevitable happened. The flagstaff crashed to the ground as a result of powerful gusts during a summer storm. Not surprisingly, Roger Harwood of

Plattsburgh was one of the first to visit the island after the storm. By the time the mast came down, Roger had already been working on the island on his own for over 4 years, fighting a seemingly impossible battle to keep the poison ivy and brush at bay so that the area around the monument would be visible and accessible.

Quoted in an article by Jeff Meyers of the Plattsburgh Press Republican, Harwood stated, "This Island has a special place in my heart. This flagpole should either be removed and protected at a museum or restored and returned to the island."[1]

Roger Harwood took this photo of the original flagstaff shortly before it fell.

The task would be easier said than done.

The flagstaff sat in pieces on the island for a year before it was finally removed from the island. Local legend and maritime salvager Capt. Frank Pabst was hired to remove the broken mast from the island. Roger Harwood had already removed the smaller pieces so that they would not be stolen or damaged by vandals.

There was much talk about preserving this important piece of local history and tradition. Would the Crab Island flagstaff receive the attention it warranted now, after its destruction at the hands of nature?

By the summer of 2001, the pieces were in storage at Point au Roche State Park. There did not seem much hope that the staff would ever be restored. I traveled to the park with Roger Harwood at the time; he was crushed to see it in this state.

Crab Island flagstaff at Point au Roche State Park. Photos by the author.

Shortly after our visit, another Press-Republican article appeared, again by Jeff Meyers. Entitled "Historic Flagpole in limbo: 1903 marker for Battle of Plattsburgh still lies broken," the story told how "the state has no immediate plans to repair a historic flagpole..." and quoted a state official as saying that the project didn't fall into the State Park's budget. The state had hired a conservator to take a look at the wreckage. A rough estimate of thirty thousand dollars (not including returning it to the island) was made to restore it to usefulness.[2]

Prospects for restoring the flagstaff were bleak at best.

Then, in typical Crab Island history "up and down" fashion there appeared a ray of hope. In March 2002, another Meyer's article heralded "Man takes a stand for flagpole."[3] A New York State Electric & Gas employee, John Rock, had read the story of the flagstaff and taken up its cause to his superiors and state officials. Rock wanted to restore the flagpole with a combination of volunteer labor and private funds. At last there seemed to be hope that, once again, the flag of the nation they died for would fly over the final resting place of the heroes of Crab Island.

John Rock was determined. The flagstaff would return to Crab Island. Yet another individual was willing to work to accomplish what state agencies could not seem to do on their own.

Rock, a long-time employee of NYSEG, convinced his employer to take on the daunting task of restoring the rusted pile of metal to its former glory. The flagstaff was in desperate shape. Broken parts had to be replaced, what could be salvaged needed sandblasting and restoration. The entire structure would have to be painted its original white color. The entire bottom section, consisting of a number of two-inch pipes surrounding one large pipe, was hopelessly rusted away and would need to be replaced.

The project began when NYSEG moved the pole from Point au Roche to the Booth property on South Junction Road. Rock was somehow able to negotiate through the complicated relationship between the New York State DEC, Office of Parks, Recreation and Historic Preservation, and Thousand Island Parks. The actual restoration work was overseen by officials of Thousand Island State Parks.

Over the summer of 2002, volunteers from NYSEG, Loya's Welding, Stay Brothers, and the community worked on the project. Their goal was to have the massive flagstaff on the island by the anniversary of the Battle of Plattsburgh- September 11.

Plattsburgh residents watched the project with much anticipation while local media kept the public informed. By the end of August, the work was essentially complete. Looking much like it did when new; the historic mast was ready to be moved to the island. Another enormous obstacle remained- how to get the 100' structure in place on Crab Island.

It is not easy moving a several ton, 100-foot long steel structure. Moving it across the stretch of Lake Champlain to the island and then erecting it in place required considerable planning and initiative. John Rock and his dedicated team of volunteers were up to the task, however. Their original hopes of having the pole on site by September 11 were dashed when it proved impossible to secure a large enough helicopter by that date.

On the morning of September 13th, largely due to the efforts of Plattsburgh Mayor Dan Stewart, a large Army National Guard twin-rotor Chinook helicopter arrived at Plattsburgh's City Beach to pick up the flagstaff. Earlier in the week, Luck Brothers had carefully moved the pole by truck to this place where the helicopter could land.

The Crab Island Flagpole is moved to the Plattsburgh City Beach for transport by a waiting Army National Guard helicopter. Photos courtesy of John Rock.

Mayor Stewart had appealed to NY Governor George Pataki, who asked the National Guard to consider lending a hand. The Guard decided they could take on the job, using the experience as a training exercise. Residents along the lake watched in amazement as the huge helicopter carefully lifted the staff from its place near the beach. John Rock and Roger Harwood were on hand to photograph the historic flight. Harwood took local television news crews to the island in his boat. Rock went straight to the island to await the big moment. Incredibly, the skilled pilot was able to negotiate the dangling flagstaff into the clearing, avoiding entanglement in the huge oaks and pines that surround the small clearing. On the ground, NYSEG and Parks officials in hard-hats watched the dramatic scene.

The Crab Island Flagpole dangles beneath the New York Army National Guard Chinook helicopter on its way across Cumberland Bay. Photos courtesy of John Rock.

On only his second try, the pilot was able to place the end of the mast into its setting on the ground. Anticipation built as the crews prepared to secure the massive tower. Then, suddenly, heartbreakingly, something went awry. Just as the crew prepared to release the staff, a gust of wind broke the hoist. The top of the pole collapsed and came crashing to the ground. Fortunately, no one was injured as the massive top-section came down.

The huge helicopter hovers just above the treetops while on the ground crews try to align the base of the flagstaff into its proper location. Photos courtesy of John Rock.

Left: The helicopter over Crab Island moments before the collapse of the pole. Above: The flagstaff lies broken, but not seriously damaged on the ground. Photos by Roger Harwood.

Hearts sank. As the ground crew anxiously took stock, the realization came that Old Glory would not wave from the mast today. The flagstaff was damaged but not seriously. Fittings were broken and the pole was bent in places, but those pieces were quickly removed and repaired. Disappointed but undaunted, Rock and his fellow volunteers left the island still determined to accomplish their task.

It was not quite a year later, on August 22, 2003, that Rock and company succeeded in erecting the massive flagstaff. Coincidentally, local media personalities Gordie Little and Calvin Castine had arranged to have Roger Harwood take them on a tour of the island that day. They happened upon the historic scene and videotaped the event step by step.

Using only manual labor, with a system of winches and pulleys attached to a nearby tree, the enormous mast was pulled upright. Soon the flagstaff was secured by steel cables. Within a few minutes, the nation's flag flew high over the island for the first time in decades. There were tears of joy as the dozen or so workers and onlookers cheered the successful effort.

Above: August 22, 2003- the Crab Island flagstaff is successfully erected on its original location at the southwestern end of the island. Four photos courtesy of John Rock.100 years after it was first erected, the Crab Island Flagstaff once again hoists the nation's flag high above the graves of the war dead buried here.

Left: John Rock and Roger Harwood. Right: the Flag is hoisted high above Crab Island for the first time in decades. Photos by Linda Harwood. Below: The Flag flies high above the trees, October 2003. Photo by the author.

IX. Crab Island Today:
Modern-day Caretakers of the Island
(1915-1965)

In a scene that illustrates the long military history of the Champlain Valley, a U.S. Air Force KC-135 makes its final approach to the runway at PAFB. Valcour and Crab Islands are visible through the cockpit window. Photo by Philippe Colin.[†]

Exactly why Thomas Connolly and his family left Crab Island in 1915 remains another of the secrets of Crab Island. We know that his wife, Elizabeth died in 1919, and Thomas himself passed on in 1925. Both were buried in Plattsburgh's Mt. Carmel cemetery.

This writer has been unable to find any information on the fate of the island between the time of Connolly's departure and 1929. It does not appear another caretaker was hired. After a brief period of attention, Crab Island National Military Park was allowed to slide into another long period of neglect.

In 1929, it would appear that any hopes of returning a caretaker to the island were permanently shattered. Official Plattsburgh Barracks Quartermaster Inventory logs show "Building No. 58, Designation- Caretaker's Cottage, Capacity- 1 Caretaker" was "Destroyed by fire 2/5/29." It was signed by J. Underwood, Captain. QMC. Evidently the house was destroyed; additional documents state that the Wood and Coal Shed, Stable, Chicken-house, and Storehouse were salvaged.[1] It would seem of little consequence that these outbuildings were not burned also. The island essentially had been abandoned.

There are unverified accounts of work on the island by the Civilian Conservation Corps during 1936, but I have yet to determine what, if anything of consequence was done at the time.

It would be the 1950's before the island would get any attention at all. The changes that began when the U.S. Air Force assumed control of Crab Island in 1953 are fascinating to relate.

Within a year of Plattsburgh Air Force Base's establishment in 1953, plans were underway to convert the island back to a park. This time, however, it would become a place where base personnel could take their families for recreation, picnicking and perhaps, camping. By May 1956, considerable work had been accomplished.

Crab Island, however, continued to keep her secrets during this time. Witness this puzzling notation from the minutes of the "380th Air Base Group Weekly Staff Meeting" dated 14 May 1956. It reads:

> "4. Crab Island: The next project in the way of clean-up will be Crab Island. As soon as the weather permits, personnel will live on the Island until it has been cleaned up. Major Bennett will be the officer in charge. The personnel will live at the caretaker's house on the island. Food service will provide the food and M/Sgt Carr will cook the meals." [2]

We have already established that the Caretaker's house was destroyed by fire on May 5, 1929. What building were the minutes referring to here? This writer believes it must have been "Sanborn Lodge."

A 20'x 30' structure, known unofficially as "Sanborn Lodge" had been built on the island (we know very little about this building, but all indications are it was a rough, crudely built structure). A letter dated 15 May 1956 from the Base Commander, Col. Immanuel J. Klette, refers to the lodge, and shows the significance he placed on the work there. Entitled "Crab Island Rehabilitation" it stated:

"1. It is my desire that the rehabilitation of Crab Island proceed at a maximum pace to insure that its recreational facilities are available for personnel of this base during the coming summer season.

2. The first project to be undertaken by your organization is to make a livable facility for a troop detachment on Crab Island. This will include minimum rehab of the lodge, latrine facilities and water pump. The work will be done by troop labor... It is desired initially to repair roof and wall leaks in the lodge, provide it with window screens and screen doors and provide some shelving and table facilities. Additionally, temporary wiring should be provided and a small generator set up at the lodge...

3. It is recommended that you commence shipping materials for this rehab immediately...

4. You are also to set up a program to take place as soon as possible for eradication of poison ivy and also for insect control. [a hand-written notation of "Gotta love that Poison Ivy" is beside the Colonel's signature]." [3]

Official base documents listing projects in the works show ongoing activity at Crab Island. Some of the notations merit listing:

> "820th Air Base Group Weekly Staff Meeting [undated]: 'Lt. Col. Weaver stated that the trailers are to be brought to Crab Island before Saturday night. The Air Police squadron will be in charge of clean-up on the Island this week-end. Lt Col. Weaver instructed Maj. Johnson to insist that the mess tent and living quarters on Crab Island be maintained in a clean, orderly manner.'"

> "820th Air Base Group Weekly Staff Meeting [16 August 1956] Crab Island Project: 'Commended Maj Haskins and his entire squadron for the excellent job done this past weekend. The Operations plan revealed a great deal of careful planning and coordination. The next squadron to spend the weekend on the Island will be Headquarters Squadron. Lt. Col Weaver advised that trailers will be dispersed on the Island. He also indicated that a survey is being made regarding the possibility of a lighting system for Crab Island...

> Some progress has been made on this project but there is still much more work to be accomplished. All squadrons with the exception of Food

Service will now furnish personnel for this project on weekends…Both first sergeants and squadron commanders will accompany the troops on weekends. Departures will be early in the morning taking necessary box lunches for all and return will be in time for the evening meal at the Mess Halls. Chaplain Mennen will make arrangements for Catholic and Protestant services Sundays on the Island. '"

"Week ending 28 Sept. 56: Crab Island: Renovation continued with detailed help from squadrons over the weekend. Each organization doing his part, such as construction and building in rest area." [4]

In October of the same year, the report stated:

"Clean-up still in progress. Project will continue until approximately 1 November."

Work was not completed by the following summer as stated in the Colonel Klette's original letter. It appears much was done, however. We have found the remains of the fireplaces erected for picnickers amidst the thick underbrush. It appears a good part of the southern end of the island was cleared.

On October 12, 1957, a story appeared in the Plattsburgh Press-Republican entitled

"Crab Island 'Paradise' Progressing." It stated "work will continue for several years" but that "some areas of the island are expected to be ready for use next summer." It mentioned the picnic area referred to previously and referred to "Sanborn Lodge," declaring that it was named for Brig. Gen. Kenneth O. Sanborn. A particularly fascinating paragraph followed under the heading "Happy Goats."

Linda Harwood inspects the remains of an unfinished recreational fireplace erected by the Air Force on Crab Island. Photo by the author.

"...goats, imported because of their fondness for poison ivy, were still reported chewing their way across 16-acre Crab Island... Originally the island was stocked with only 5 goats. The next time amazed base officials counted there were ten. The exact count now is being kept a closely guarded secret." [5]

The article was accompanied by a photo of two airmen with a "goat-eed Crab Island resident." Colonel Klette had mandated something be done about the poison ivy! One has to credit the Air Force for coming up with such an innovative (and ecologically sound) solution.

Alas, all the efforts of the Air Force on Crab Island were in vain. By the end of 1957, it appears the military simply gave up their "rehabilitation" of Crab Island. It seems to have happened quite suddenly, too. At least one of the picnicking fireplaces on the island was left incomplete, never to be finished. We do not know if any airmen ever brought their families to the island for rest and recreation.

The United States Air Force had completed their time as Caretakers of Crab Island.

There were a number of recreational fireplaces erected by the Air Force on the southern end of Crab Island, most either were never completed or were partially dismantled. Photos by Linda Harwood.

Notes:

[†] An excellent summary of Plattsburgh Air Force Base history can be found at Philippe Colin's *Plattsburgh AFB and the 380th BW* <http://www.philippecolin.net/380thBW.html>.

[1] Plattsburgh Barracks: Quartermaster inventory documents. Caretaker's Cottage specifications, Building No. 58 Reported to C.O. by letter, that date, file 6.00.971x600.6 for 1929.

[2] Minutes: 380th Air Base Group Weekly Staff Meeting- 14 May 1956

[3] Letter: Col. Immanuel J. Klette, USAF, Base Commander- 15 May 1956

[4] Minutes: 820th Air Base Group Weekly Staff Meeting- August/October 1956

[5] Plattsburgh Press-Republican: "Crab Island 'Paradise' Progressing" October 12, 1957

X. Crab Island Today:
Modern-day Caretakers of the Island
(1965-1988)

In 1965, the Air Force informed the U.S. General Services Administration they did not want, and certainly did not need, Crab Island. The last time the island had a practical use for defense purposes was in 1814. Despite their gallant attempts to utilize Crab Island as a recreation "paradise" in the 1950's, one can hardly fault the Air Force for making this decision.

It fell to GSA to determine what to do with the property. An inspection was made of the island by an appraiser and a "Realty Specialist" on January 5, 1966, in the dead of winter. Incredibly, the document that resulted, a "Notice of Surplus Determination" went out to potential buyers of the island with no mention of the graves from 1814. Jim Bailey tells us the document did not even mention the Crab Island Monument! [1]

Local government agencies were offered the island. Unfortunately, there were no takers. This is probably because the island is isolated and fairly difficult to access. In addition, GSA required a plan for maintenance of the island were it to be purchased by a public entity. [2]

GSA opened up bidding to the general public on July 17, 1967. This place, an island with a military burial ground, designated a National Military Cemetery by an Act of Congress, was going to be auctioned off to the highest bidder, monument, graves and all!

On December 5, 1967, it was announced that the high bidder was Mr. Edward Troise of Pennsylvania. Though the bid was reported as being $20,200. the actual high bid was $40,200, still a pittance when one considers what the government had put into the island over the years. The Troise family kept the island in the family for over 15 years, doing very little with the property. That turned out to be a very good thing, for the Plattsburgh Press-Republican, complaining of the sad state of the monument, reported in July 1975, "'there will likely be some kind of development at some future time,' and that among the offers turned down were one from The Atomic Energy Commission. It seems they were interested in "developing the island as a site for a future power generator." Imagine, the Crab Island Nuclear Power Facility! To this writer, that scarcely seems better than the offer from Las Vegas developers to build a casino on the island, also mentioned in the piece.

Undoubtedly, in an effort to reassure readers, Mr. Troise was quoted in the article as stating, "...the proper authorities would be contacted to make sure the monument would be removed to a place where it could be preserved." Officials would be given the opportunity to remove the Crab Island Monument from Crab Island... Given the condition of the monument at the time (and the condition it remains in today) one wonders about the benefits of doing this. As odd as that prospect sounds, one wonders if the monument itself would have fared better had it been relocated. Forrest Cleland, who authored the piece, hit what seems to me to be the height of understatement when he concluded- "... the significance of the marker would certainly be diminished if it were removed to a museum and the resting place of the war dead were one day disturbed by the whirring of a roulette wheel or the click of glasses in a casino cocktail bar." [3]

The time did come when the Troise family decided it was time to sell off the island. Another battle was to erupt around Crab Island.

$150,000- will subdivide. So read the listing in local papers. For the Troise family, it was time to see a return on their investment. The year was 1985; Crab Island was again for sale.

This time the public would raise their voices. The Ad Hoc Committee for a Public Crab Island was formed. This group consisted of dedicated members of many local civic organizations. The Committee was co-chaired by Mr. James Dawson and one James G. Bailey. Jim Bailey; the Plattsburgh City Historian, is, in this writer's view, one of the Caretakers of Crab Island.

Dawson, Bailey and the Ad Hoc Committee were determined that Crab Island revert to public ownership. After deciding against taking the GSA to court for the original private sale in 1967, a dogged effort was made to convince New York State to purchase the island at the price Troise wanted. After initially being rebuffed in their efforts, the group finally convinced the state to attempt the purchase. The island was appraised by the state. The Office of Parks, Recreation, and Historical Preservation [referred henceforth as OPRHP] would buy Crab Island.

Serious complications ensued, however. A wealthy New Jersey resident; Mr. Walter Jakubowski, decided he wanted Crab Island. He was willing to pay for it, too. Jakubowski offered $190,000. for the island. This was well above the asking price, and, considerably more than the state could pay due to the appraised value of the island. Troise accepted the larger sum and Jakubowski became the new owner. [4]

By now the public was informed, largely due to the efforts of Bailey, the Ad Hoc Committee, and the news media. Pressure was relentlessly applied on the state to enter into negotiations with Jakubowski. Jim Bailey kept up his public campaign to make sure everyone knew of the history associated with Crab Island. One of the most touching and poignant of these efforts took place on Memorial Day, 1986. Nothing I could write would better show Baileys' commitment and devotion to the island and his respect for the graves there.

As a project for American Education Week, the students of the Broad Street School in Plattsburgh released helium-filled balloons with a card attached asking the finder to contact them. Bailey found one on Crab Island. His response to "Jonella of Broad Street School" is telling. It is reproduced here with permission:

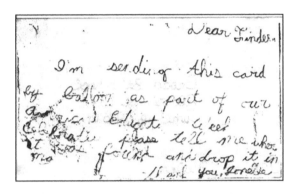

Above: The balloon-launched card found by Jim Bailey on Crab Island in 1986. Left: Bailey's handwritten response to Jonella of Broad Street School.

Memorial Day, 1986
Crab Island in Plattsburgh Bay

Dear Jonella of Broad Street School:

Here is your balloon-carried postcard back to you. We saw it drifting over and landing nearby, but until today we couldn't get it back. Mr. Bailey, Plattsburgh City Historian, paddled out as a Memorial Day activity to do some more searching about Crab Island (or St. Michael's Island) history-- trying to locate our graves.

As you say in that game "I see something", he was red hot.

While he was so close, we sent him a message to look down for your balloon card. We didn't shout or moan, because he's deaf and wouldn't hear. It was an extra-sensory kind of message. Anyway, he looked down at just the right time and spotted your card among the poison ivy vines.

We're glad the balloon card is a project of American Education Week. You and your school-mates can do some educating about America's history right here in Plattsburgh. Because, honestly speaking, the past generations have not done very well by us.

We are MacDonough's sailors who died aboard his ships Sunday morning September 11, 1814 defending Plattsburgh and the United States against a British invasion.

Commodore MacDonough was a shrewd naval commander and despite being outgunned and outmanned that day, we won a great victory which won the War of 1812 against Britain. He was a kind and decent officer, too. He had all of us who were killed in battle, including the British, properly buried. Of the 53 American seamen who died in the naval battle, 4 were officers and were taken to the village cemetery for burial. You can see that burial site from your Broad Street School window. The remaining 49 of us, together with about 80 British sailors, were buried here on Crab Island-- the closest land to the naval battle--in mass graves. MacDonough did not have the time or money to erect stone markers. It wasn't until 1843 that a group of Plattsburgh veterans collected enough money to put up the gravestones you see in Riverside Cemetery today.

No stone markers ever got put up over our graves out here.

About 1900, local people finally persuaded the U.S. government to do something. By then, however, our graves were so overgrown that they couldn't be found on this 40 acre uninhabited island. So the government erected a memorial flagpole at the south end of the island in 1903, and a granite shaft near the north end in 1908. They also built a caretaker's cottage, a windmill to pump lake water to the cottage, a wharf, and had paths cut all around the island. By 1909, it was quite an attractive park-- MacDonough National Military Park was its formal name. At least people at that time knew we were here even though they couldn't find the exact grave sites. We were proud that, finally, we were remembered.

Your teachers have told you that true learning takes a lot of repeating. Unfortunately, the U.S. government did not truly learn the lesson of our sacrifice. The government's overseers of the military park island did not keep it in shape. Over the last 80 years, all the work done in 1900-1909 has been ruined by neglect. The flagpole is hopelessly rusted. The wharf is broken up by the ice. Careless campers burned the cottage down in 1965. Two of the four bronze plaques have been stolen off the granite monument. The paths are completely overgrown. The biggest blow to us was in 1967 when the government formally abandoned the whole island and sold it to an out-of-state land speculator. He didn't do a thing for 19 years: now, in 1986, he wants to sell it to someone else for a good profit, maybe for dividing up for a bunch of camps or houses. Our graves!

There's hope that the State of New York will pick up the fumble of the U.S. government and buy back the island. The Committee for a Public Crab Island has been formed to try to rekindle Plattsburgh's remembrance of our sacrifice. 172 years is a long time to go without a gravestone!

Your balloon may not have traveled the farthest in distance from Broad Street School, Jonella, but it has taken the record for time! From September 1814 we send greetings to you and all in Plattsburgh on Memorial Day 1986-- hopefully the beginning of real Memorial Days for us.

Thomas Butler   Spokesman for the 49 American on Crab Island
Quarter Gunner on MacDonough's Flagship, The Saratoga

With the island now in the hands of the Jakubowski interests, it would seem there was not much more that could be done. Mr. Jakubowski wanted the island and he had been willing to put up a lot of money to get it. To his credit, he started getting the island cleaned up soon after the purchase. Plattsburgh's well-known entrepreneur Frank Pabst was commissioned to work on Crab Island and start investigating ways of opening it up to the public. Pabst, whose popular tour boat, *Juniper*, had been plying the waters of Plattsburgh and Valcour Bays, investigated promoting the island as a place for "rustic camping" and using the island for ski and snowmobile touring. Moorings would be set out for boats at the island. [5]

The momentum to return the island to public ownership was strong, however. The Town of Plattsburgh voted new zoning regulations for Crab Island in recognition of its rich history. These regulations, it would seem, would serve to prevent Jakubowski from developing the island extensively. Before long, pressure was applied upon the state to exercise its right of eminent domain. Eminent domain would entail forcing the owner to sell at a fair market price. It is not something used often and it is used reluctantly. There is a long tradition of fighting for the rights of individual property owners in the North Country. Yet, public sentiment was strong that the federal government was wrong in selling the island in the first place. It kept coming back to the graves... Crab Island was the burial ground of some 149 British and American seamen from the War of 1812. They had died in battle here- in Plattsburgh. Did these veterans deserve recognition? It had been decided long ago that they did. As Jim Bailey stated so eloquently in his letter to Jonella, however, "honestly speaking, the past generations have not done very well by us." Perhaps it was finally time to make things right.

The State of New York determined it was in the best interest of the people to take the island by eminent domain.

On January 11, 1988, papers giving the state ownership of the island were filed. Mr. Jakubowski was paid $210,000., some $20,000 above what he paid for Crab Island.[6] The people of the State of New York were the new stewards of Crab Island.

Jim Bailey was pleased. His work, however, was not finished. The Ad Hoc Committee, together with local news media and other concerned and involved citizens had done much to preserve the special and unique character of Crab Island. The island still desperately needed attention.

On February 28, 1988, Bailey conducted a tour of the island. It was some six weeks after the state acquired Crab Island. Forty people walked across the frozen lake to the island. The visit was covered by Press-Republican Staff Writer Mitch Rosenquist. Bailey pointed out that the four bronze plaques from the monument were no longer on the island. Two were in safekeeping in Plattsburgh; the other two were in the possession of the island's last owner. The tour group noted the sad state of the monument. They were also taken to a location that Bailey thought was as likely a spot for the burial site as any.[7]

Jim Bailey was doing what he could to bring the plight of Crab Island to the fore. In the fall of 1988, Bailey wrote "The Forgotten Graves of Crab Island." Published in The Antiquarian, the official journal of the Clinton County Historical Association, the "Forgotten Graves" is a wonderful, well-written account of the story of Crab Island. Up until now, it is believed to be the only published work specifically dealing with the islands' history. Jim Bailey and the Clinton County Historical Association graciously allowed the republication of the "Forgotten Graves" on the America's

Historic Lakes website. That Crab Island tour was 14 years ago. The location of the graves has still not been established. The monument is in somewhat better condition than it was at that time. The broken gate has been fixed. The trees growing through  the fence have been removed. The area around the monument has been cleared of poison ivy and extensive brush. The path from north to south has been restored. It was not the State of New York, however, that performed these necessary tasks. It was yet another Caretaker of Crab Island.

Jim and Anne Bailey. Photo by the author.

Notes:

[1] James G. Bailey, "THE FORGOTTEN GRAVES OF CRAB ISLAND" (The Antiquarian-Fall 1988, Allan Everest, Editor Clinton County Historical Association, Plattsburgh, NY) 14. Also republished with permission: America's Historic Lakes, <http://www.historiclakes.org/ccha/bailey1.htm > May 2001.

[2] Ibid.

[3] Forrest Cleland: 1812 War Monument in Disrepair. Plattsburgh Press-Republican: July 15, 1975.

[4] James G. Bailey, "THE FORGOTTEN GRAVES OF CRAB ISLAND" (The Antiquarian-Fall 1988, Allan Everest, Editor Clinton County Historical Association, Plattsburgh, NY) 14. Also republished with permission: America's Historic Lakes, <http://www.historiclakes.org/ccha/bailey1.htm > May 2001.

[5] Frank Pabst. Personal communication to Roger Harwood. June 2002.

[6] James G. Bailey, "THE FORGOTTEN GRAVES OF CRAB ISLAND" (The Antiquarian-Fall 1988, Allan Everest, Editor Clinton County Historical Association, Plattsburgh, NY) 14. Also republished with permission: America's Historic Lakes, <http://www.historiclakes.org/ccha/bailey1.htm > May 2001.

[7] Mitch Rosenquist: 40 Visit Crab Island on 1st Tour since state takeover. Plattsburgh Press-Republican: February 29, 1988.

Top: Most of Crab Island is overgrown and thickly wooded. Bottom: The area around the flagpole has been cleared and is well maintained by Roger Harwood. The contrast is quite striking. Photos by the author.

XI. Crab Island Today: Modern-day Caretakers of the Island (1988-Present)

Visitors to Crab Island today will find the island in as good a condition as it has been in many years. There are still many problems, some quite serious. As Jim Bailey pointed out in "The Forgotten Graves of Crab Island"[1] back in the Fall of 1988, the monument still needs pointing, the four bronze plaques are still missing (although they are now on display at the Clinton County Historical Association Museum), and with the exception of one large sign identifying the monument's significance, there is no signage on the island. There are large gaps in the monuments' mortar, and of course, the eagles remain headless.

Yet, Crab Island can be accessed by a careful boater (there is no dock or wharf), and watchful visitors can pick their way up the shore to the monument. It is still important to avoid the occasional poison ivy plant along the shore to the clearing on the west side.

Once ashore, the area around the monument stands out in sharp contrast to the heavily forested section behind it. As this recent photo shows, the monument is surrounded by a neat, well-cropped, grassy section. The fence, long since covered with a thick

layer of rust, at least is standing erect. Trees and thick vines no longer grow through the openings, entwining themselves through its open sections. The gate, once off its hinges and on the ground, has been restored to its proper place. There is a path, not very wide, but clearly defined nonetheless, from the clearing along the western shore past the ruins of the cottage. Poison Ivy no longer grows within the narrow clearing, but in the springtime, the path does blossom with beautiful (and protected) wildflowers. The path continues to the area where the massive naval style flagstaff stands once again. This area, too, has been cleared of incredibly dense brush and thicket. Yet, nothing has been removed from the area but trash and blow-down. There is obvious evidence that whoever did this work has an enormous respect for Crab Island.

Roger Harwood, of Plattsburgh, NY, is a retired Industrial Arts teacher. He is a long-time volunteer firefighter, avid boater and an accomplished diver. He is also the latest Caretaker of Crab Island. For some ten years now, Roger has lovingly maintained the area around the monument and the flagstaff. He has mowed the grass and repaired the fence. He has cleared the trees, poison ivy and brush from within the fenced in area. He has cleaned up the blow-down after lake storms. Roger is not an employee of the State of New York. He has done this work, on his own time, at his own expense, because it needed to be done. Roger has a no-nonsense approach to why he comes here. He will tell you "someone needs to do it."

Roger Harwood working years ago at the Crab Island Monument. Photo by Linda Harwood.

The work is not easy, nor has it always been appreciated or welcomed.

Four years after the State of New York took possession of Crab Island very little had changed. It seemed the little island was doomed to a continued future of neglect. Other than the one large sign (it is a nice sign) just to the north of the monument, for all intents and purposes there was no indication that state ownership had made any difference whatsoever.

Jim Bailey had suggested back in that hopeful year of 1988 "signs to note the natural and historic features--e.g. the invalids' battery at the north tip-- could be erected at a modest cost." He then went on to state his strongest desire- "the most important need is for OPRHP to send its archaeologist to pinpoint the burial trenches, and then to fence in and clearly mark the area." Bailey lamented that there was nothing on the island noting the fact that 149 American and British sailors are buried somewhere on this tiny piece of ground.

As of this writing in August 2003, there is still nothing telling the tale of Crab Island to visitors or passers-by. The graves have not been located, and other than the monument, itself suffering the ravages of time and neglect; nothing remains to honor the memory of the fallen heroes of Macdonough's and Downie's fleets.

Roger Harwood loads his riding mower and takes it to Crab Island. He now uses a larger boat.

Roger Harwood does what he can. Each week or so, he puts his specially customized power mower into his little boat and travels the two or so miles from his home to Crab Island. Just as he has for the past ten years. Sometimes he has help, usually it is

Linda his wife; but mostly Roger works alone here. Then again, perhaps Roger is not alone as he works on Crab Island. There are at least 149 men buried in unmarked graves here. They have been ignored, dishonored and forgotten by too many for too long. Roger Harwood remembers them. Perhaps they are working alongside him. That just may be another of the Secrets of Crab Island.

Roger Harwood at work on Crab Island.

Roger Harwood and the author at the Crab Island Monument, October 2003. Photo by Jim Dooley.

Notes:

[1] James G. Bailey, "THE FORGOTTEN GRAVES OF CRAB ISLAND" (The Antiquarian-Fall 1988, Allan Everest, Editor Clinton County Historical Association, Plattsburgh, NY) 14. Also republished with permission: America's Historic Lakes, <http://www.historiclakes.org/ccha/bailey1.htm > May 2001.

XII. The Future: What Will Become of Macdonough National Military Park?

On the morning of September 11, 2001, while the world watched in horror the events unfolding in New York, Washington and Pennsylvania, a group of men made their way up the western shore of Crab Island. They knew of the anguish the nation was experiencing at that moment, doubtless most would have liked to have been at home with their families at that difficult time, yet they had come for a very special purpose.

Veterans gather at the Crab Island Monument, September 11, 2001. Photo courtesy of John Tomkins III.

These men, many of them veterans of other American wars, had come to honor the seamen who perished at the Battle of Plattsburg and are buried at Crab Island. Clinton County Historical Association Director John Tomkins captured that moment for us with Roger Harwood's camera. It is one photo that speaks volumes.

In the last 13 chapters of The Secrets of Crab Island, this writer has tried to explain the significance of this tiny limestone isle in the midst of Cumberland Bay. We have explored the island's history from prehistoric times until today. We know that other generations have tried to honor those buried here. Unfortunately, to some extent, their efforts may have seemed futile. Nothing less than an Act of Congress called for the creation of a national military park here. Over the last century, the United States government and the government of the great State of New York each authorized the expenditure of hundreds of thousands of taxpayer dollars for the preservation and maintenance of Crab Island.

Yet, a private citizen voluntarily mows and cleans up the trash. He does it because it needs to be done.

It is not the intention of this work to point fingers or assign blame. It IS the intention of this piece to promote action. Something needs to be done about Crab Island. Jim Bailey said it in 1988. Nothing was done. It is my sincere hope that something positive will result from my stating it in 2002. Wiser men than I have stated what needs to be done. Much of the work needed has been listed elsewhere in this missive. I will not venture to repeat it here. It is obvious; however, that something needs to be done about Crab Island.

Ceremonies at Crab Island, September 11, 2003. Left: Veterans honor the fallen at the Crab Island Monument. Right: Roger Harwood raises the Stars and Stripes and the British Union Jack to the top of the restored Flagstaff. Photos by Philip LaMarche.

 Crab Island's tale is the story of America. Here are buried those who died defending the United States from one of the last foreign attacks on its mainland until September 11, 2001. Their graves are somewhere on the island, American and British seamen together. The United States and Great Britain have been allies in one great conflict after another since that terrible time in the Republic's early history when the two nations fought each

other. They stand together still.

There can be no better way to conclude this piece than by listing the names of those who are buried here. These men have names. They had families and loved ones. There is nothing on Crab Island to tell the world it is their final resting place.

The Crab Island Monument was decorated with a wreath and bunting when the author visited the island on July 4th, 2003. Photo by the author.

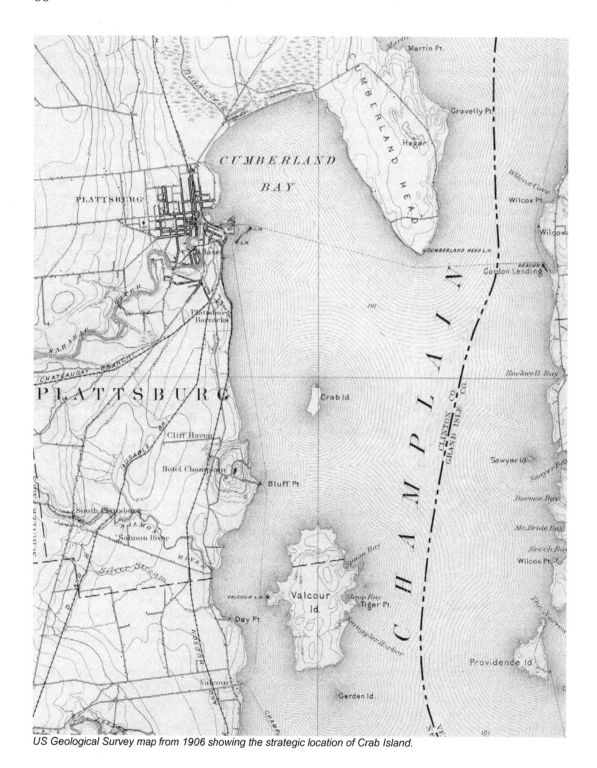

US Geological Survey map from 1906 showing the strategic location of Crab Island.

Individuals presumed buried on Crab Island*

American Dead

Thomas Butler	*Quarter Gunner*
James Norberry	*Boatswain's Mate*
Abraham Davis	*Quartermaster*
William Wyer	*Sailmaker*
William Brickell	*Seaman*
Peter Johnson	*Seaman*
John Coleman	*Seaman*
Benjamin Burrill	*Ordinary Seaman*
Andrew Parmlee	*Ordinary Seaman*
Parnel [Purnell] Boice†	*Ordinary Seaman*
Peter Post	*Seaman*
David Bennett	*Seaman*
Ebenezer Johnson	*Seaman*
Joseph Couch	*Landsman*
Thomas Stephens	*Seaman*
John White	*Ordinary Seaman*
Randall McDonald	*Ordinary Seaman*
Samuel Smith	*Seaman*
Thomas Maloney	*Ordinary Seaman*
Andrew Nelson	*Seaman*
John Sellack	*Seaman*
Peter Hanson	*Seaman*
Jacob Laraway	*Seaman*
Edward Moore	*Seaman*
Jerome Williams	*Ordinary Seaman*
James Carlisle	*Marine*
John Smart	*Seaman*
Peter Vandermere	*Master's Mate*
Jno. Ribero	*Seaman*
Jacob Lindman	*Seaman*
Perkins Moore	*Ordinary Seaman*
James Winship	*Ordinary Seaman*
Thomas Anwright	*Ordinary Seaman*
Nace Wilson	*Ordinary Seaman*
Thomas Lewis	*Boy*
John Wallace	*Marine*
Joseph Heaton	*Marine*

British Dead

Peter Jacobs	*Seaman*
William Stimpson	*Seaman*
James Austin	*Seaman*
Abraham Bean	*Seaman*
John Berry	*Seaman*
John Mitchel	*Seaman*
William Griffith	*Seaman*
James Wilson	*Seaman*
Robert Mathews	*Seaman*
Joseph Rea	*Seaman*
John McManus	*Seaman*
Daniel Capps	*Seaman*
Miles Sweney	*Seaman*
John Sald	*Seaman*
William Rose	*Seaman*
John Belse	*Seaman*
James [Liggett]	*Seaman*
Charles Labwin	*Seaman*
Alexander Morrison	*Seaman*
Charles Oatey	*Seaman*
Louis Butler	*Seaman*
Patrick McGuire	*Seaman*
John Tempest	*Seaman*
Thomas [Douie]	*Seaman*
Robert Charters	*Seaman*
William Smith	*Seaman*
James Powers	*Seaman*
Thomas Bishop	*Seaman*
William Beaty	*Seaman*
Robert Richards	*Artillery*
John Morris	*Artillery*
Philip Prangly	*Marine*
Henry Holgoud	*Marine*
Edward England	*Marine*
Benjamin Thomas	*Marine*
Philip Bohagan	*Marine*
Joseph Viscery	*Marine*

Continued on next page

American Dead

Robert Stratton	*Marine*
James M. Hale†	*Musician*
John Wood	*Musician*
John Fisher	*Boatswain's Mate*
John Atkinson	*Boatswain's Mate*
Henry Johnson	*Seaman*
Deodorick Think	*Marine*
John Sharp	*Marine*
Joseph Rowe	*Boatswain's Mate*
Arthur W. Smith	*Purser's Steward*
Thomas Gill	*Boy*
James Day	*Marine*

British Dead

Owen Green	*Marine*
Alexander Williamson	*Seaman*
William Auston	*Seaman*
Hugh Fullard	*Seaman*
Joseph Cox	*Seaman*
Edward Shelton	*Seaman*
William Loveless	*Seaman*
Daniel Drysdale	*Seaman*
William Stokes	*Seaman*
George W. Slaney	*Seaman*
John Wright	*Seaman*
John Newman	*Seaman*
Alexander Bouie	*Seaman*
Andrew Ramsay	*Seaman*
John Kirkham	*Seaman*
Stephen Moore	*Seaman*
George Erving	*Seaman*
M. McLoughlin	*Seaman*
Samuel Atkins	*Seaman*
Roger Owens	*Seaman*
James Bivin	*Artillery*
Jacob Maling	*Artillery*
William Bird	*Artillery*
John Weaver	*Marine*
James Smith	*Marine*
William Vaughn	*Seaman*
Robert Campbell	*Seaman*
John Hill	*Seaman*
John Hames	*Seaman*
Joseph Pease	*Seaman*
Daniel O'Bryan	*Seaman*
Henry McLaughlin	*Seaman*
John Radioffe	*Seaman*
John Smith	*Seaman*
Joseph Moore	*Seaman*
Joseph Stephens	*Seaman*
John Long	*Seaman*
Thomas Broadnay	*Seaman*
Mark Everhard	*Marine*
James May	*Marine*

This is a list of those killed and grievously wounded in the naval battle from Macdonough's and Downie's fleet. It was compiled from the only sources I could find to this date. It is possible that some listed here recovered from their terrible wounds. That said, given the state of medical care at the time and the difficult wartime conditions, it is unlikely. There are undoubtedly soldiers buried here also from Macomb's army on the shore. Note the list does not include officers. They were interred with honors in Plattsburgh's Riverside Cemetery.

This list is not all inclusive and certainly does contain errors. The author is confident that most of the individuals listed here are, indeed, interred on the island.

† *Revised 8/18/2002.* Boice was inadvertently left off the original listing. He was an Ordinary Seaman from the *Eagle* who died of his injuries three days after the battle. My thanks to Dr. Kevin Crisman for bringing this to omission to my attention. Dr. Crisman, the noted nautical archaeologist from Texas A&M University, has also provided the following information regarding Musician James M. Hale:

"U.S. Army Musician James M. Hale (presumably buried on Crab Island) had his wife Abigail Woodruff Hale with him aboard EAGLE when he was killed. Their two infant children had recently died, and she apparently left home and joined him at Plattsburgh in 1814; when he was sent aboard the EAGLE shortly before the battle to serve on one of the gun crews, she went with him, and ended up carrying powder to the guns (like Molly Pitcher of Revolutionary War fame). According to the story I have, she found James dead on the deck while doing so. She re-married in Plattsburgh in December and lived out the rest of her life in western Pennsylvania. One wonders whether she was able to arrange any sort of special burial for James, or if he was just laid in the ground with the rest of them."

Select Bibliography

Bailey, James G., "*THE FORGOTTEN GRAVES OF CRAB ISLAND*" (The Antiquarian-Fall 1988, Allan Everest, Editor Clinton County Historical Association, Plattsburgh, NY) also republished with permission: America's Historic Lakes, <http://www.historiclakes.org/ccha/bailey1.htm > May 2001

Bailey, James G., 1988. *Crab Island- Walking Tour of Plattsburgh City Historian*. Pamphlet.

Becker, Lawrence R., Vermont State Geologist, Fossils of the Lake Champlain Region, 5 May 2002, <http://www.anr.state.vt.us/geology/pubint.htm> (16 May 2002)

Bellico, Russell P. 1992, 2001. *SAILS AND STEAM IN THE MOUNTAINS- A Maritime and Military History of Lake George and Lake Champlain.* Fleischmanns, New York: Purple Mountain Press, Ltd.

Charbonneau, Andre. 1994. *THE FORTIFICATIONS OF ILE AUX NOIX.* Minister of Supply and Services, Canada. Parks Canada, Canada Communication Group. Translated from the original French

Colin, Philippe. 2004. *Plattsburgh AFB and the 380th BW.* <http://www.philippecolin.net/380thBW.html> (29 December 2003)

Coolidge, Guy Omeron. 1938, 1940. *The French Occupation of the Champlain Valley from 1609 to 1759.* Reprint of second edition (1989), with biographical indexes. Fleischmanns, New York: Purple Mountain Press, Ltd.

Everest, Allan S. 1981. *The War of 1812 in the Champlain Valley.* Syracuse, NY: Syracuse University Press

Fay, H. A. 1817. *COLLECTION OF THE OFFICIAL ACCOUNTS, IN DETAIL, OF ALL THE BATTLES FOUGHT BY SEA AND LAND, BETWEEN THE NAVY AND ARMY OF THE UNITED STATES, AND THE NAVY AND ARMY OF GREAT BRITAIN, DURING THE YEARS, 1812, 13, 14, & 15.* New York: E. Conrad. (Library of American Civilization; LAC 12346)

Fitz-Enz, David G., 2001. *The Final Invasion- Plattsburgh, the War of 1812's Most Decisive Battle.* New York, NY: Cooper Square Press

Hadden, James M. 1776-1777. *Hadden's Journal and Orderly Books: A Journal Kept in Canada and Upon Burgoyne's Campaign in 1776 and 1777, by Lieut. James M. Hadden, Roy. Art.* Edited by Horatio Rogers. Albany: Joel Munsell's Sons, 1884

Haviland, William A., Marjory W. Power. 1994. "The Original Vermonters: Native Inhabitants, Past and Present" University of Vermont: Published by University Press of New England, Hanover, NH

Hays, James T., David E. Mize, and Richard W. Ward, *"Guns under Lake Champlain"* (York State Tradition, Spring 1969)

Hill, Ralph Nading. 1976. *LAKE CHAMPLAIN- Key to Liberty.* Shelburne, Vermont: Shelburne Museum and The Countryman Press

Holden, James A. 1914. *The Centenary of the Battle of Plattsburg.* Albany, New York: The University of the State of New York

Lake Champlain Maritime Museum, *Geological History,* <http://www.lcmm.org/site/harbor/resource_pages/timeline/geological.htm > (16 May 2002)

Lake Champlain Maritime Museum. 2003. *Historical and Archaeological Narrative of New York Islands in Lake Champlain.* Prepared by Sara R. Brigadier and Adam I. Kane under the direction of Arthur B. Cohn. New York State Department of Environmental Conservation, Ray Brook, NY.

Lewis, Dennis M. 1994. *BRITISH NAVAL ACTIVITY ON LAKE CHAMPLAIN DURING THE WAR OF 1812.* Plattsburgh, New York and Essex, New York: Clinton County Historical Association and Essex County Historical Association

Lossing, Benson J. 1869. *THE PICTORIAL FIELD-BOOK OF THE WAR OF 1812; OR, ILLUSTRATIONS, BY PEN AND PENCIL, OF THE HISTORY, BIOGRAPHY, SCENERY, RELICS, AND TRADITIONS OF THE LAST WAR FOR AMERICAN INDEPENDENCE.* New York: Harper & Brothers, Publishers. (Library of American Civilization; LAC 14918-19)

Macdonough Commission of Vermont, The. 1914. *Macdonough Centennial-Vergennes, Vermont.* Souvenir Program

Mann, James, M.D.A.A.S. 1816. *MEDICAL SKETCHES OF THE CAMPAIGNS OF 1812, 13, 14, TO WHICH ARE ADDED, SURGICAL CASES; OBSERVATIONS ON MILITARY HOSPITALS; AND FLYING HOSPITALS ATTACHED TO A MOVING ARMY.* Dedham, MA.: Printed by H. Mann and Co.

Millard, James P. 1997, 2002. *"A Signal Victory on Lake Champlain- The Battle of Plattsburg".* America's Historic Lakes-The Lake Champlain and Lake George Historical Site.<http://www.historiclakes.org/Plattsburg/plattsburgh_battle1.htm>

Millard, James P. 1997, 2002. *"The Battle of Lake Champlain, October 11, 1776",* America's Historic Lakes-The Lake Champlain and Lake George Historical Site. <http://www.historiclakes.org/Valcour/valcour_battle.htm>

Millard, James P. 2002. "*The Secrets of Crab Island*". America's Historic Lakes-The Lake Champlain and Lake George Historical Site. <http://www.historiclakes.org/crab/crab_intro.htm>

Morgan, William James, Editor. 1972. *Naval Documents of the American Revolution. Volume 6.* Washington, D.C.: Naval History Division, Department of the Navy

New York State Commission Plattsburgh Centenary. 1914. *THE BATTLE OF PLATTSBURGH- WHAT HISTORIANS SAY ABOUT IT.* Albany, New York: J. B. Lyon Company, Printers

Palmer, Peter S. 1886-1889. *History of Lake Champlain, from its first exploration by the French in 1609 to the close of the year 1814.* New York: Frank F. Lovell & CompanyPlattsburgh Press-Republican: various issues

Silliman, Benjamin.1820. *Remarks Made on a Short Tour Between Hartford and Quebec in the Autumn of 1819.* New Haven. CT: S. Converse.

The Court martial of Captain Daniel Pring and the Officers and Men Employed in the Squadron on Lake Champlain. August 18-21, 1815 on Board H.M.S *Gladiator* in Portsmouth Harbor. Public Records Office, Kew Gardens, London.

Tuttle, Mrs. George Fuller. 1909. *THREE CENTURIES IN CHAMPLAIN VALLEY- A COLLECTION OF HISTORICAL FACTS AND INCIDENTS, Tercentenary Edition.* Plattsburgh, NY: Saranac Chapter, D.A. R.

Index

Visiting Crab Island...

Crab Island is publicly owned land- the property of the people of New York. It is also a very special, unique place that merits respect and consideration. Keep in mind the island is covered with Poison Ivy. It is also the home of protected fauna and flora. Overnight camping, metal detectors and digging are strictly prohibited on the island.

Made in the USA
Columbia, SC
16 March 2019